Devil's Advocates

DEVIL'S ADVOCATES is a series of books devoted to exploring the classics of horror cinema. Contributors to the series come from the fields of teaching, academia, journalism and fiction, but all have one thing in common: a passion for the horror film and a desire to share it with the widest possible audience.

'The admirable Devil's Advocates series is not only essential – and fun – reading for the serious horror fan but should be set texts on any genre course.'
Dr Ian Hunter, Reader in Film Studies, De Montfort University, Leicester

'Auteur Publishing's new Devil's Advocates critiques on individual titles... offer bracingly fresh perspectives from passionate writers. The series will perfectly complement the BFI archive volumes.' **Christopher Fowler,** *Independent on Sunday*

'Devil's Advocates has proven itself more than capable of producing impassioned, intelligent analyses of genre cinema... quickly becoming the go-to guys for intelligent, easily digestible film criticism.' *HorrorTalk.com*

'Auteur Publishing continue the good work of giving serious critical attention to significant horror films.' *Black Static*

DevilsAdvocatesbooks

DevilsAdBooks

ALSO AVAILABLE IN THIS SERIES

Antichrist Amy Simmonds

Black Sunday Martyn Conterio

The Blair Witch Project Peter Turner

Cannibal Holocaust Calum Waddell

Carrie Neil Mitchell

The Company of Wolves James Gracey

The Curse of Frankenstein Marcus K. Harmes

Dead of Night Jez Conolly & David Bates

The Descent James Marriot

Halloween Murray Leeder

Ju-on The Grudge Marisa Hayes

Let the Right One In Anne Billson

Macbeth Rebekah Owens

Nosferatu Cristina Massaccesi

Saw Benjamin Poole

The Silence of the Lambs Barry Forshaw

Suspiria Alexandra Heller-Nicholas

The Texas Chain Saw Massacre James Rose

The Thing Jez Conolly

Witchfinder General Ian Cooper

FORTHCOMING

Don't Look Now Jessica Gildersleeve

The Fly Emma Westwood

Frenzy Ian Cooper

In the Mouth of Madness Michael Blyth

Psychomania I.Q. Hunter & Jamie Sherry

Scream Steven West

Devil's Advocates

The Shining

Laura Mee

Acknowledgments

First and foremost, I would like to thank John Atkinson at Auteur for his patience, encouragement and sound editorial guidance. I am grateful as ever to Ian Hunter and Johnny Walker for their enthusiasm for this project, and I am very lucky to have had James Fenwick to help me wade through a rather intimidating pool of existing work on Kubrick, his take on which was most appreciated. The team at the Stanley Kubrick Archive at UAL's Archives and Special Collections Centre were very accommodating and helped me to make the most of my time spent researching there. Thanks to my colleagues at the University of Hertfordshire, who have been incredibly supportive, and especially to Howard Berry, who has been both a sounding board and a truly valuable resource. Analysing *The Shining* as part of a horror course I taught at Phoenix, Leicester prompted a number of interesting ideas from groups equally passionate and critical about the film—thank you all. Finally, huge thanks to friends and family who put up with my obsessions and absences while I was writing, and especially to Ben Marchini, Caitlin Shaw and Charley Meakin for their limitless love, support, proofreading and ass-kicking. This book is for them.

N.B. Citations of sources with the prefix 'SK' refer to documents held at the Stanley Kubrick Archives, London College of Communication, University of the Arts London, accessed in February and March 2016.

First published in 2017 by
Auteur, 24 Hartwell Crescent, Leighton Buzzard LU7 1NP
www.auteur.co.uk
Copyright © Auteur 2017

Series design: Nikki Hamlett at Cassels Design
Set by Cassels Design www.casselsdesign.co.uk
Printed and bound in Great Britain

All rights reserved. No part of this publication may be reproduced in any material form (including photocopying or storing in any medium by electronic means and whether or not transiently or incidentally to some other use of this publication) without the permission of the copyright owner.

British Library Cataloguing-in-Publication Data
A catalogue record for this book is available from the British Library

ISBN paperback: 978-1-911325-44-4
ISBN ebook: 978-1-911325-45-1

Contents

Introduction 7

Chapter 1: Kubrick and Horror 17

Chapter 2: Adapting *The Shining* 35

Chapter 3: Genre and Themes 57

Chapter 4: Release, Reception and Cultural Legacy 81

Conclusion 99

Bibliography 103

INTRODUCTION

The Shining, Stanley Kubrick's adaptation of Stephen King's bestselling novel about a family falling apart over a cruel winter season in a haunted Colorado mountainside hotel, is widely acclaimed as one of the greatest horror movies ever made. It is celebrated for its unusual, artistic aesthetic, its mysterious, puzzling narrative, a permeating sense of claustrophobic dread, and a stellar performance by Jack Nicholson as possessed Jack Torrance, whose deranged 'Here's Johnny' has spawned countless imitations. The film was eagerly anticipated; the late Stanley Kubrick was a celebrated and popular filmmaker with a reputation for precise and total control over his films from inception to exhibition, and *The Shining*, as his first horror film, was an exciting prospect for audiences. The same was true for Kubrick himself, who had long expressed an interest in making a horror film. His widow, Christiane, has said of his interest in the genre: 'When he was younger, he decided he was going to make a horror film that was so scary, he would advertise by saying that you'd get your money back if you could sit all the way through' (in *Staircases to Nowhere* [Berry, 2013]). That she adds 'and then he grew up' speaks volumes about the kind of horror film *The Shining* is—avoiding gimmicks, its terror is instead largely found in strangeness, slow suspense and the lingering threat of violence and the supernatural, but punctuated with the odd sharp shock which hits like an axe to the chest.

It took time for the film to become recognised as the essential and effective horror movie it is regarded as today, however. It was released to fairly flat reviews, which found its narrative confusing, its eccentric performances irritating, and argued that Kubrick had butchered King's novel, only succeeding in demonstrating his disinterest in the genre and his ineptitude in making a horror film. For many critics, *The Shining* was simply not frightening. The re-evaluation that has taken place subsequently has, to some extent, sought beyond considerations of genre in highlighting the film's value, focusing on the adaptation of King's book, Kubrick's auteur status and filmmaking style, and analysis of its 'deeper' meanings, rather than situating it—as much of its audience has—in the context of horror cinema. These approaches are significant, and they offer useful frameworks for a closer look at the film, but it is important that they are considered in parallel with its position as a horror film. This book brings together these ideas to offer a study of *The Shining* in its rightful place.

THE SHINING SYNOPSIS

Jack Torrance (Jack Nicholson) takes a job as a winter caretaker at the grand and remote Overlook Hotel, moving his wife Wendy (Shelley Duvall) and son Danny (Danny Lloyd) with him for the season. Jack is a recovering alcoholic, a former teacher and now a writer, and looks forward to the quietness and isolation of the hotel, high in the mountains and miles from the nearest town, to get started on a new project. The Overlook's manager, Stuart Ullman (Barry Nelson), warns Jack that previous caretakers have struggled with the hotel's solitude, including a man named Charles Grady, who succumbed to cabin fever and killed his wife and daughters and then himself. Jack is unperturbed by the story. Arriving at the hotel as it closes for the season, the family meet resident chef Dick Halloran (Scatman Crothers), who bonds with Danny over their shared psychic abilities, which he calls 'shining'. Danny has had horrifying visions which made him fearful about coming to the hotel; Dick confirms the Overlook has a troubled history but reassures him the shining is 'just like pictures in a book' and not dangerous—yet cautions the boy to stay out of room 237.

Cut off from civilisation by the Overlook's mountainous location and, as the weather starts to turn, deep snow, Jack and Danny encounter strange visions and figures, including Grady's dead daughters, who appeal to Danny to 'come and play…forever and ever'. Tensions rise between the Torrances as Jack becomes increasingly withdrawn, struggling with writer's block and preoccupied with the hotel and his responsibility to it. He connects with apparitions from the hotel's glamorous past, including bartender Lloyd (Joe Turkel), whom Jack treats as a confidante, and butler Delbert Grady (Philip Stone). Danny, ignoring Dick's advice, is drawn to room 237 and assaulted by a spirit. Wendy pleads with her husband to leave the hotel—which, with Jack now dedicated to staying with the hotel and its ghosts, only makes him angrier. Grady, after insisting that Jack has 'always been' the Overlook's caretaker, warns him that Danny has made contact with Halloran in an attempt to seek help, and urges him to 'correct' his wife and son. Jack destroys the radio and cuts the wires in the hotel's snow plough, trapping the family. He threatens Wendy, but she manages to knock him unconscious and lock him in a store cupboard. Grady apparently lets Jack out, and he pursues Wendy and Danny with an axe. Halloran arrives to check on the family, but Jack immediately murders him. Danny escapes and leads his father in to the Overlook's enormous hedge maze, where he tricks him, leaving Jack lost to die in the freezing snow while Danny and Wendy flee in Halloran's Snowcat. A final glimpse at the Overlook's empty corridors reveals rows of photographs on the wall, including one with Jack holding court among revellers at a grand party. The caption reads 'Overlook Hotel, July 4th Ball, 1921'.

1 *Lost in the maze*

***

Principal photography for *The Shining* was shot at EMI-Elstree Studios and MGM-British Studios in Borehamwood. A second unit team, headed by Stanley Kubrick's brother-in-law Jan Harlan, filmed exterior shots for the opening credits in Montana, and of the Timberline Lodge in Mount Hood, Oregon, which stood in for the Overlook in long shots establishing its remote location. Enormous interior sets of the Overlook Hotel's grand spaces and corridors took over the entire studio lot at Elstree, filling sound stages and repurposing offices and workshops, utilising the backlot for the hotel's exteriors and its huge water tank for a shot of an elevator spewing torrents of blood. The sets were connected, helping to create the effect of a working hotel on the scale of the Overlook, and enabling disorienting shots of characters moving between the staff-only and guest areas. The interconnection offered the ideal space for showcasing the exceptionally smooth, low-angled tracking shots of Garrett Brown's newly invented Steadicam—particularly effective in scenes in which Danny rides his tricycle from the Colorado Lounge around back corridors and through the kitchen.

Stories of Kubrick's obsessive perfectionism, not only at the helm of a shoot but also in editing, release and exhibition, had become commonplace. But interviews with crew members suggest a respect for working with a professional who was less concerned with schedule and more with getting things right—a 'hard taskmaster' who carefully planned and executed every element of his work and expected the same of the people working with him. Cinematographer John Alcott described Kubrick as 'very demanding. He demands perfection, but he will give you all the help you need if he thinks that whatever you want to do will accomplish the desired work' (in Lightman 1980: 844). Nonetheless, *The Shining*'s shoot was notoriously arduous, and the intended time spent shooting at Elstree nearly doubled, running for just under a year between May 1978 and April 1979, with lengthy development and editing periods bookending its protracted production. Long filming days and countless takes on hot, practically lit sets took their toll on the schedule, and the director's and actors' frustrations. The production made its indelible mark on Elstree studios, the ground damaged by the salt which doubled for snow, and soundstages left roofless by a large fire which all but gutted the stage housing the grand Colorado Lounge set, further delaying *The Shining*'s completion and the start of shooting on *The Empire Strikes Back* (Kershner, 1980), due to take over the stage.[1] Critics were quick to connect the event to Kubrick's reputation: 'It wasn't an army that marched through Elstree, but it was the cinema's closest one man equivalent', Harlan Kennedy wrote in a piece for *American Film* coinciding with *The Shining*'s release (1980: 49). Aligning the secretive production with the vague themes and unclear narrative that had puzzled some early reviewers, Kennedy painted a picture of auteurist calculated chaos, which demonstrated the context in which many first watched the film:

> Not surprisingly a Kubrick production is defined by its paradoxical extremes. Violence and science, passion and pedantry, serendipity and calculating perfectionism combine in an operation that often seems military in its comprehensiveness. Kubrick's famous long production schedules are part of the same syndrome. From first conception to final attentions—including the vetting of individual release prints and projection quality in the cinemas—*a Kubrick film is a Kubrick film*. (1980: 52, emphasis added).

As a Kubrick film, and his first in five years, anticipation was high. As a horror film, *The Shining* did not stand a chance.

STUDYING *THE SHINING*

Robin Wood, writing in a revised edition of *Hollywood from Vietnam to Regan*, explained the 'striking omission' of Stanley Kubrick's work from his original study. He acknowledged that constructing a narrative for Kubrick's career was challenging, and that he had rarely connected with his films – even while identifying himself as 'a great admirer' of *The Shining* (2003: xxxviii). Wood's admiration is sufficient to include stills of a menacing Jack and terrified Wendy, which fill the first illustrated page of his prologue. The caption 'patriarch on the rampage, wife on the defence' connects the film to Wood's critical and theoretical concerns, but exclusion of *The Shining* from his seminal essays on horror cinema is, to borrow the author's term, striking, and demonstrates the difficulty finding its fit within the genre. 'The American Nightmare' sets out a method for understanding the 'return of the repressed' in 1970s genre films, an oft-cited model for horror (psycho)analysis where the monster is a potentially sympathetic 'Other' produced by the bourgeois white patriarchy, with radical political potential. In 'Horror in the 80s', Wood criticises the genre's reactionary turn toward the conservative and horror's more ambiguous motivations for its monsters. Its release straddling the decades, and the narrative refusing to offer obvious themes and motivations which would align it clearly in either direction, *The Shining* remains absent from Wood's analyses because of its uncomfortable association with the genre trends of either era, and its muddy identification with any national cinema.

The Shining is often only briefly considered elsewhere—or otherwise omitted entirely—in significant scholarly writing on horror cinema. Peter Hutchings mentions the film in his discussions of music (2004: 146), performance (153) and gender (155) in horror. Andrew Tudor includes it in a list of titles which demonstrate a shift in horror's antagonists to the 'psychotic' human monster (1989: 128), and among the varied films featuring haunted or haunting families (75, 100, 176); Reynold Humphries connects this to the horror of the family home (2002: 103). Brigid Cherry offers a short consideration of its use of the uncanny (2009: 92) and colour (80), and Rick Worland briefly acknowledges *The Shining*'s familial horror themes and unusual take on Gothicism in his history of the genre (2007: 102-103). Kendall Phillips mentions it in connection with horror films featuring 'dangerous young people' (2005: 122), justified in the author's later acknowledgment that readers have suggested the film warrants consideration because of Danny's abilities. (197). Despite the significance of gender in *The Shining*'s themes, it does not quite fit the models under consideration in Carol Clover's *Men, Women and Chainsaws* (1992), receiving only cursory mentions. Kubrick's film is eschewed entirely in Mark Jancovich's *American Horror* (1994), which instead offers detailed discussion of King's novel (21-22) (perhaps on account of the film's status as a British-American co-production), and it is absent from the chapters featured in his comprehensive edited collection *Horror: The Film Reader* (2002), as it is from another substantial collection on the genre (Gelder 2000). Elsewhere, the film is dismissed as 'essentially a vision of [its] maker'—positioning it as a Kubrick film, rather than a noteworthy inclusion in the contemporary horror canon (Wells 2000: 94), and a curious anomaly, a not-quite-horror-film in a chapter on genre aesthetics (Dickstein 2004). Matt Hills's *The Pleasures of Horror* explores the genre's wider place in popular culture and examines its enduring appeal for audiences; *The Shining* is not discussed further than drawing from viewer anecdotes about watching it (2005: 84, 204), despite Jack's 'Here's Johnny!' face leering from the book's cover.

The Shining has not often been considered within serious studies of the horror genre in depth, despite frequent acknowledgement of its popularity and thus its significance, lending some weight to the idea that Kubrick produced a horror film which functioned outside of the genre's recognised codes and conventions. Its exclusion from studies of American or British horror films highlights a further problem, symptomatic of the difficulties faced in easily defining national genre cinema, and especially in locating co-productions within these categories. Lacking the obvious 'Britishness' found in the rural horror of a film like *The Wicker Man* (Hardy 1973), or the easily identifiable studio brand of a Hammer film, *The Shining* is a film 'British' enough to have changed the working face of an entire UK studio, but perceivably 'American' in its themes and aesthetic, made by a celebrated American auteur who had been living and working in the UK for going on twenty years. Kubrick worked across genres and did not specialise in horror, and *The Shining* has been simultaneously welcomed as an artistic, creative interrogation of the horror of the human psyche, and critiqued as a particularly ineffectual horror film.

It is perhaps little surprise then that *The Shining* does not sit comfortably within broader studies of horror, despite a number of articles and chapters on the film's themes and aesthetic which examine it (as effective or otherwise) within the genre (Jameson 1981,

Cramer 1997, Lutz 2010, Wright 2011, Model 2012). Instead, the film largely finds its academic merit in valuable examinations of cult followings (Egan 2015, Hunter 2016), adaptation case studies exploring the process of translating King's novel to the screen (Jenkins 1997, Magistrale 2003, Browning 2009, Wright 2011, Pezzotta 2013, McAvoy 2015), and, chiefly, within the context of Stanley Kubrick's work in auteurist approaches (Titterington 1981, Nelson 1982, Naremore 2007, Webster 2011, Kolker 2011) and chronicles of production history and minutiae (LoBrotto 1997, Baxter 1997, McAvoy 2015c). Roger Luckhurst's 2013 study does tease out a number of the film's generic conventions by connecting *The Shining* to previously released horror films, and offering a detailed textual analysis of the film's major themes, focusing on the trope of the maze and psychoanalysis. *The Shining* has been the subject of a great deal of academic work, but not all of it approaches the film as part of popular horror cinema.

Playing Devil's Advocate

Popular, non-academic writing on horror has had no difficulty aligning *The Shining* with the genre. Alan Jones, even while making the familiar accusation that Kubrick, spurred on by artistic arrogance and with no grasp on the genre, produced a 'Kubrick film first and a horror film second' (2005: 146), includes *The Shining* within 'the canon' of horror classics, acknowledging its defence by fans as a 'celebration of the perverse beauty of horror' (ibid.). Kim Newman's appreciation of the film is mixed, matching critical and audience 'incomprehension', but recognising its effectiveness in leaving so much unexplained (1988: 226-227). Russ Thorne suggests that viewing the film is 'akin to a religious experience in cult circles' (2014: 24), while Tarja Laine insists that '*The Shining* remains arguably the scariest and the most impressive horror film ever made' (in Schneider 2009: 274). Jack Torrance even replaces *The Exorcist*'s Regan MacNeil as the cover star of a 2016 edition of Steven Jay Schneider's *101: Horror Movies You Must See Before You Die* (joining another Schneider book, 2008's *Horror Cinema*, on which Nicholson also features)—a sign of the film's sustained (or even increasing) popularity. Daniel Olsen's collection (2015) of new and reprinted essays and interviews illustrates *The Shining*'s enduring fan-scholar crossover appeal, as well as the endless possibilities for obsessive analysis, and research undertaken by academics and keen viewers.

While a number of these sources echo tensions found in confused critical responses to *The Shining* (to which I will return in a later chapter), the frequent inclusion of the film in non-academic writing on horror suggests something of a clash between popular audience perceptions and academic ones. Many scholars are perhaps hesitant to engage with it as a successful and enduringly popular horror film when it takes such a seemingly unusual approach to the genre, and when it can instead be pored over for hidden meaning, or dissected as an artistic, auteurist vision. This of course speaks volumes about the low-culture status often afforded horror—the work of a 'serious' filmmaker like Kubrick sits uncomfortably within the genre and is therefore skimmed over within its studies, while those more interested in Kubrick's oeuvre can instead ponder over what he was trying to get across by using base horror as a vehicle for loftier pursuits. Even in celebrating the film's achievements, its generic associations are often downplayed. For example, in a panel discussion, '*The Shining*: Horror's Greatest Achievement?', held at the BFI to coincide with the film's 2012 extended cut release in the UK, the chair pushed for discussion of *The Shining* as 'more than just a genre movie', and insisted on looking 'beyond genre' to instead consider themes including family tensions. Speaker Kim Newman takes umbrage with this, observing that 'it is possible to find profundity in ghost stories…just as it's possible to find banality in art movies'.[2] Newman is correct, of course. Furthermore, the attempt to separate genre and text only highlights the centrality of the film's themes—including familial and generational tensions—to horror cinema more broadly.

This not only suggests issues regarding the policing of culture, taste and genre by deeming *The Shining* either 'too arty' for horror or the genre 'too crass' for Kubrick to work in seriously or successfully. It also ignores common consensus and fails to engage with the film in the way a large sector of its audience has—as a popular, effective, scary movie. *The Shining* has been the subject of immersive cinema events and special screenings, featured in seasons of Gothic and horror cinema, and has had theatrical re-releases in recent years, its continued popularity with horror, cult, and general audiences warranting repeated considerations and opportunities to engage with the film on the big screen. Frequently, it tops or ranks highly in lists of horror films and frightening moments compiled by the likes of *Empire*, *Total Film*, *Time Out* or *Film4*, and it has featured in magazines including *Scream*, *Diabolique* and *Fangoria*, or on niche horror sites such as *Dread Central* and *Bloody Disgusting*. A study measuring audience heart rates as they watch horror films has even claimed *The Shining*'s final moments to be the most frightening on film (Murakami 2013), supporting research which labelled it the 'perfect scary movie' according to a complex mathematical formula (BBC 2004)—the commercial intentions of the sponsors behind such studies emphasising its mainstream appeal (Play.com and Sky Movies, respectively). Attempts to move beyond considerations of the film as part of the contemporary horror canon overlook the way its audiences have embraced the film, and *The Shining* deserves consideration as a legitimate part of popular horror cinema, not something which wholly transcends it or misses its marks.

FOOTNOTES

1. For further reading, Vincent LoBrutto (1997) offers a detailed discussion of *The Shining*'s production history, compiling anecdotal information about its development and Kubrick's working practices. First-hand accounts from the film's crew, which offer valuable technical insights in to the production at Elstree as well as details of working with Kubrick, can be found in the documentary *Staircases to Nowhere: Making Stanley Kubrick's 'The Shining'* (Berry, 2013) made as part of The Elstree Project (theelstreeproject.org), which compiles oral histories of those who worked at the studio in its heyday.
2. '*The Shining*: Horror's Greatest Achievement?' (Panel Discussion), BFI Southbank, 7th November 2012, available at https://www.youtube.com/watch?v=bsF6XhoxePs (accessed 10/10/16).

Chapter 1: Kubrick and Horror

Many horror films have been made by directors considered masters of the genre, and many directors have worked almost exclusively within horror. Fans seek out work helmed by particular filmmakers—Carpenter, Craven, Romero, Fulci, Argento, Bava (and in more recent years, maybe Wan, Zombie, Roth, Wingard or West)—who were prolific in their horror production and produced their most popular work in the genre. Often, it is not just their association with horror but what they have brought to it, their personal styles and identifiable stamps, which appeal. Cronenberg's body horror weirdness, Carpenter's synth scores, Argento's murder-as-art setpieces, Romero's political satire, Zombie's retro scuzz, Roth's gross-out homages and so on, mark many out as horror auteurs (or aspiring auteurs, at least). Their names guarantee a particular set of expectations around the content and style of what a viewer chooses to watch, and their films continue to inspire new genre filmmakers, their influence on horror's evolution ever apparent. At the same time, a significant number of the most popular horror films have been made by directors who worked across genres, and found success through commercial and/or artistic endeavours—Michael Powell, (*Peeping Tom*, 1960—the controversial film which pre-empted the slasher cycle infamously all-but-ending his career), Roman Polanski (*Repulsion*, 1965, *Rosemary's Baby*, 1968), Nicolas Roeg (*Don't Look Now*, 1973), Brian De Palma (*Carrie*, 1976), Richard Donner (*The Omen*, 1976), William Friedkin (*The Exorcist*, 1973) and John Landis (*An American Werewolf in London*, 1981) among them.

Stanley Kubrick, of course, fits within this second group as a filmmaker who worked across genres and was not best known for horror. Rather, he sits alongside the group; it is difficult to associate Kubrick and his work—or at least, its reputation—too closely with that of anyone else. Few filmmakers have received such devoted critical and scholarly attention, and arguably no director has been discussed, analysed and obsessed over in such reverent terms. With a filmmaking career spanning almost fifty years but resulting in only thirteen features, each more eagerly anticipated than the last (and, no doubt maddeningly for his aficionados, the gap between releases growing in later decades), Kubrick had a reputation as an auteur of the rarest kind, able to secure both critical and commercial success while retaining artistic vision, credibility, and autonomy from studio control. This reputation has swelled to near-mythical proportions since his death in 1999, post-completion but pre-release of his final film *Eyes Wide Shut*.[3] Stories of Kubrick's perfectionism, obsessive attention to detail, and absolute control over much of his work (as writer, producer and director) have been rewritten and repeated *ad nauseum* alongside close scrutiny of his films' themes, aesthetic and meaning. During his career, and then posthumously, this has contributed to a cult following and critical consensus of Kubrick as one of the greatest filmmakers of all time. The idea of Kubrick as the ultimate auteur romanticises his films to the point where they are seen to transcend generic identification and commercial appeal, embodying 'such a stylistic and conceptual density that they are capable of stimulating even the most parochial of critical tastes' (Nelson 1982:1).

Kubrick's growing reputation was aligned with the popularisation of auteur theory; it is understandable that his films have been approached in this way, and few would argue that his status is not largely deserved or his films not great. But frequently, such considerations distance Kubrick and his work from industry contexts, elevating them beyond genre and commercial necessity (and, ironically, the idea of the auteur as a marketable 'brand'), when this may actually provide a useful approach to understanding his films. Dennis Bingham's reception study of *The Shining* suggests that the lukewarm critical response to the film (to which I will return later) can be attributed in part to the tensions between notions of the auteur and generic expectation. Released at the tail end of a period of unprecedented freedom and creativity in filmmaking in the 1970s, *The Shining* clashed with both a shift back towards the packaging of popular styles and the name value of the director: 'the auteurist romance whereby directorial genius "transcends genre" eventually gave way to a business practice that valued auteur directors mainly for their proficiency at delivering generic goods in a deluxe edition' (Bingham 1996: 285). This shift from Renaissance to artistically-informed mainstream production is frequently (and more clearly) illustrated using the careers of the Hollywood 'movie brats' and the release of films like *Jaws* (Spielberg, 1975) and *Star Wars* (Lucas, 1977). But it is not unreasonable to suggest that, following the initial critical and commercial disappointment of *Barry Lyndon* (1975), Kubrick's work with Warner Bros. at the turn of the 1980s may have been caught up in similar expectations as the major studios refined their commercial directions and realigned at least some level of artistic control. The fact that a Warner Bros. executive, John Calley, sent Stephen King's manuscript to Kubrick for consideration as a potential project certainly supports this idea (Naremore 2007: 187).

While he might have generally defied expectation and convention, Kubrick worked within genres, not entirely beyond them, and genre has played a significant part in understanding many of his films, even when he has been credited with revising them. *2001: A Space Odyssey* (1968) is retrospectively seen to have redefined science fiction, making serious work in the genre not only possible but popular, and paving the way for the likes of *Alien* (Scott, 1979), *Blade Runner* (Scott, 1982) and *Close Encounters of the Third Kind* (Spielberg, 1977). *A Clockwork Orange* (1974) provides an altogether more dystopian sci-fi vision. *Paths of Glory* (1957) and especially *Full Metal Jacket* (1987) are notable examples of the (anti-) war film, and he also made a period drama (*Barry Lyndon*), a historical epic (*Spartacus*, 1960), and noir-ish crime films (*Killer's Kiss*, 1955 and *The Killing*, 1956). *Dr Strangelove or: How I Stopped Worrying and Learned to Love the Bomb* (1964) spliced science fiction, war film and comedy, and *Eyes Wide Shut* is an erotic drama. Kubrick's films, while never entirely conforming to their conventions, are still recognisable within generic categories; they 'inhabit and deconstruct genres rather than exemplify them' (Hunter 2015: 277).

The Shining can be understood in a similar fashion; a horror film made by a man who had 'no fixed ideas about wanting to make films in particular categories' (Kubrick, in Nelson 1982: 4) and who picked at, reordered and reshaped the features of those categories. The initial critical disdain for the film can be understood in part alongside the rejection of the idea of Kubrick as a lowly 'genre director', and further attributed to the low cultural status awarded to horror: 'while the idea of a great film artist 'reduced' to making horror movies eclipses the myth of the auteur whose brilliance overcomes the lowliest of genres, it does reproduce auteurist disdain for the popular audience', Bingham argues, before himself contributing to said disdain: 'contempt for "vulgar" tastes could be felt in the film itself, Kubrick's rendition of a base genre' (1996: 285). This rhetoric is not as immediately evident in the reception of the horror films made by other genre-ambivalent directors—but without the same status as Kubrick, they are not subject to the same scrutiny. There is little evidence that Kubrick was trying to undermine horror with *The Shining*, exactly (although plenty to suggest he was parodying a number of its tropes) and the film should not be considered on a lesser plane than his other films on account of its popularity within a discredited genre. Furthermore, it is not unreasonable to suggest that Kubrick, so frequently disassociated from horror, actually had a solid grasp on the genre and a stylistic approach which leant itself to horrific effect.

While Kubrick's films might more easily be categorised (at least, for the purposes of arbitrary taxonomy) as 'war films', 'epics', 'science fiction', etc., many feature horrifying elements—the dystopian setting and shocking violence of *A Clockwork Orange*, the threat of nuclear war and the prospect of life after it in *Dr Strangelove*, the trauma of combat in *Full Metal Jacket*, the deviant sexuality of *Lolita* (1962) or *Eyes Wide Shut*. Kubrick may not be known as a horror filmmaker, and his credentials for making a horror film were challenged by a number of voices within the genre (not least King himself), but some of his thematic and stylistic tropes fit it quite well, providing plenty of opportunity to shock or unnerve a willing audience. Eschewing a number of mainstream conventions, Kubrick films are celebrated by many and rejected by others on account of the same features—ditching 'surface realism, depth of characterisation, and fast action, in favour of distanced contemplation, elliptical narrative, and spectacle' (Hunter 2015: 277). These things at once appeal to the viewer willing to engage with and figure out Kubrick's work, while turning off many more, but they also lend themselves to the attributes of some of the most successful horror stories. Surrealism and spectacle, disorienting aesthetic, the suspenseful slow build, confusing storytelling which retains mystery and refuses to explain everything to an audience who are instead required to fill in the gaps with imagination or puzzle solving—all are evident in *The Shining*, and in Kubrick's broader body of work. In theme and tone, form and style, the director's auteurist tropes are evident in the film, and rather than prove Kubrick as a horror 'amateur', they very much demonstrate how he was in fact a suitable match for the genre.

COLDNESS, BLACK HUMOUR AND THE GROTESQUE

Kubrick's detractors have often complained of a 'coldness' in his films, an 'arctic spirit', as critic Pauline Kael described it (in Naremore 2006: 4), a distance from the subject at hand which positions characters and narrative in front of the viewer for examination, rather than encouraging explicit identification with protagonists. Kubrick avoids the overtly melodramatic (which provides a challenge for suggestions that *The Shining* can be understood as a family melodrama—see Metz 1997), avoiding emotional cues and rendering 'tone' or 'mood' enigmatic. Cinematographic choices, like the use of a wide angle lens, single point perspective and tracking shots further add to this disconnection by drawing attention to his films *as films*—detailed and carefully constructed sets, an artistic flair for colour and pattern, symmetrically framed shots, all captured as a work of art. The result is often a distanced study of behaviour, rather than an emotional emphasis on character association. These same approaches are used in *The Shining*, unsurprisingly leading to similar complaints as Kubrick discourages any obvious empathy with Wendy or Danny as the narrative's victims. Stephen King argued that the film is 'cold', as opposed to his 'hot' novel, citing a lack of character development and observing that, literally, 'the book ends in fire and the movie in ice' (quoted in Greene 2014).

The perceived coolness of Kubrick's adaptation not only matches his broader style, but contributes to a subtle black humour. Writing some years before *The Shining*, Peter Wollen described Kubrick's portrayed worlds as 'dehumanised', suggesting 'his pessimism is cold and obsessive', and further arguing that 'for Kubrick, the bitter-sweet easily spills over into the grotesque and into black farce':

> …the fight with fire-axe and fire-pole between Davy and Rapalo in *Killer's Kiss*, in which a roomful of tailor's dummies are hacked to pieces by huge swipes, limbs and heads flying everywhere; Nikki's conversation with the negro car-park attendant in *The Killing*; the ping-pong before Quilty's murder in *Lolita*, the grotesque Pentagon war-room sequences in *Dr Strangelove*. Expressionism is pushed toward Surrealism – bizarre juxtaposition, macabre undertones, the triumph of the irrational. (1963: 128-129)

The difference with *The Shining*, of course, is that this grotesquery, dark farce and unnerving surrealism is played much closer to the surface, the macabre *overtones* employed as a function of the genre in which Kubrick was working. Was he writing two decades later, Wollen might have included in this list: Jack and Wendy's staircase scene, the tense, racist conversation with Grady in the red bathroom, the use of fairytale tropes and mythology, the dog-man giving a tuxedoed partygoer a blow job, or another well-dressed ghost (Norman Gay), bloodied but jolly, raising his glass to Wendy and exclaiming 'Great party, isn't it?'.

2 'Great party, isn't it?'

"Grotesque" is often employed in discussions of horror, particularly when referring to exaggerated, gross or gory images of the body (or its various forms of decay or destruction). But it is more broadly understood as being associated with 'both the carnivalesque and the terrifying—at one extreme with gross-out comedy and at the other with the monstrous, the uncanny, or the supernatural', and furthermore, in visual contexts, as a rhetorical mode akin to parody and defined by 'tension between laughter and some unpleasant emotion such as disgust or fear' (Naremore 2006: 3). As with his films' supposed coldness, Kubrick's use of the grotesque leaves his audience unnerved, unsure of how to respond and unsettled by any potentially inappropriate primal reaction like laughter. We can laugh comfortably at *Dr Strangelove*'s war room sequences, knowing it to be an acceptable response to the genre of movie we are watching— laughing is a gut reaction to things we find humorous. (It also clearly demonstrates that we get the joke, and so takes on an additional righteous function for audiences of political satire.) Obviously, it is not uncommon for horror to be funny or to provoke laughter—the 'splatstick' humour of 1980s splatter films, for example (see Brophy 1986), or the nervous laughter that might cathartically follow jumping at an unexpected shock. In the case of *The Shining*, though, the grotesque humour risks further alienating (or at least unsettling) an audience—for what is the appropriate response to blackly humorous representations of domestic violence or child abuse?

The Shining does not offer us catharsis from the effect of its various horrors through humour (although it is hard to take the penultimate shot of Jack, frozen in the labyrinth, as anything other than comical); rather, it finds a lot of its horror in unnerving us by encouraging laughter at its grotesque presentations, many of them through Nicholson's performance, and his presentation of Jack as simultaneously terrifying and ridiculous. In one of the film's most frightening sequences, Jack follows Wendy up the grand staircase of the Colorado Lounge as she backs away in terror, swinging a baseball bat and begging him to stay back. Jack mocks his wife, raising his voice to a squeak and copying her speech, exaggerating his movements in grotesque parody. He even attempts to be funny: 'Wendy, darling, light of my life, I'm not gonna hurt you'—Wendy swings—'you didn't let me finish my sentence. I said, I'm not gonna hurt you. I'm just gonna bash your brains in. I'm gonna bash 'em right the fuck in.' He laughs at his own joke, before lowering his voice and taunting: 'Wendy, gimme the bat, Wendyyyy.' Later, the violence of Jack breaking down the door with his axe is juxtaposed with his jokey 'Wendy, I'm home', and his now-famous references to Johnny Carson ('Here's Johnny!') and the Three Little Pigs ('not by the hairs on your chinny chin chin? Then I'll huff, and I'll puff…'). This is even more alarming—a grotesque parody of family life reminding us that this snarling, dogged, would-be-killer is, first and foremost, still a husband and father who, in another life away from the Overlook, might watch late-night talk shows with his wife and read nursery rhymes to his young son.

During the earlier scene at the Gold Room bar, when Jack confides in Lloyd after Wendy accuses him of abusing Danny in room 237, Nicholson's mugging is even more obvious in static close-up. Initially, the camera stands in for Lloyd, summoned by Jack offering his soul for a drink. He surveys the empty room and then addresses us directly as he notices: 'Little slow tonight, isn't it?' before laughing maniacally. A reverse-shot reveals Lloyd looking back: 'Yes, it is, Mr Torrance. What'll it be?' Cutting back to Jack, the camera is now to Lloyd's left, recording the exchange rather than playing Lloyd's part in it. After instructing the bartender to 'set 'em up' so he can 'knock 'em back' ('Here's to five miserable months on the wagon, and all the irreparable harm that it's caused me', he toasts, raising his bourbon), Jack assures Lloyd that he would never hurt Danny: 'I wouldn't hurt one god damn hair on his head. I love the little son of a bitch! I'd do *anything* for him. Any fucking thing for him.' He looks side to side, checking he is definitely alone with Lloyd, before leaning in conspiratorially and beginning a confession: he had hurt him once, 'completely unintentional, coulda happened to anybody' (he looks directly at the camera for a split second, implicating the audience as 'anybody'). Jack suddenly gets angry, raising his voice, violently flailing his arms, providing actions for his rant: 'It was three god damn YEARS AGO. The little FUCKER had thrown all my papers all over the floor, all I tried to do was PULL HIM UP.' A pause, he calms and switches back to quiet explanation: it was, he dismisses with a wave of his hand and a glib tone, 'a momentary loss of muscular coordination'.

The sudden switch between Jack's cartoonish expressions and sitcom banter with Lloyd to his angry outburst, and the swift change back, perfectly illustrates the juxtaposition between the violent and the comic in *The Shining*. It is quick, alarming, and broken up with a glance that implicates us in its humour, that dares us to laugh one last time before Jack imitates breaking his son's arm by force. It is horrific precisely because we are encouraged to find it funny. As a horror film, *The Shining* foregrounds the blackly comic style Kubrick commonly employed. Complaints of tonal coldness connect to a discomfort with the grotesque, the black humour in *The Shining* refusing its audience 'the comfort of secure response', and reminding us that 'there is always something potentially comic about horror, and horrible about comedy' (Naremore 2006: 11).

THE UNCANNY AND THE UNEXPLAINED

Any suggestion that *The Shining* demonstrates Kubrick's contempt for the horror genre fails to take into account his fascination with a number of subjects aligned with it—the dark side of human nature, the unconscious, and the paranormal. King's book provided Kubrick the opportunity to explore these obsessions, and—although not specifically chosen on account of this—appealed to his belief in ESP (Ciment 1980: 473). While stories which explore the darker human psyche feature in much of his work (*A Clockwork Orange*, *Eyes Wide Shut*, *Lolita*, *Full Metal Jacket*), *The Shining* perhaps features the clearest example of Kubrick's interest in exploring the unconscious and the uncanny. Kubrick and co-writer Diane Johnson expanded on themes in King's book using psychoanalytic literature – notably Freud's essay on the uncanny *Das Unheimliche* and Bruno Bettelheim's *The Uses of Enchantment*, which applied Freud's theories to myths

3 Jack addresses us as Lloyd...

4 ...and as spectators

and fairy tales. Many analyses of *The Shining* use this framework in exploring the film's hidden meanings, and it is not my intention here (nor is it productive) to regurgitate complex psychoanalytic interpretations of the film when much interesting and detailed work already exists (Hoile 1984, Nolan 2011, Model 2012, Trigg 2015, McAvoy 2015 and others). However, I think it is useful to briefly consider the general ambiguity of the themes and narrative in this context. The refusal to provide clear explanations and tidy conclusions, the avoidance of exposition, the long silences and emphasis on visual rather than verbal language, and the film's 'coldness', can all be attributed in part to the desire to unnerve an audience through evoking the uncanny, a feeling of the strangely familiar representing unconscious, repressed or forbidden desires and impulses.

This 'strangely familiar' is configured in repetition, a feeling of things that are the same and yet somehow different. In *The Shining*, this occurs in a number of ways. There is a sense throughout of history repeating itself, of the Overlook's horrible past returning to haunt this new family, through Danny's shining, in Jack's alcoholism, in the threat of him becoming violent again, and in the suggestion that he has 'always been' the caretaker (a title which takes on new meaning after his conversation with Grady), or that he might 'correct' his family just as Grady 'corrected' his wife and daughters. Visually, it exists in symmetrically framed shots, the patterns of the maze and the indistinguishable corridors of the hotel, and in the frequent use of mirrors and mirror images. There are also instances of uncanny doubling in the characters—the Grady girls (sisters, but very alike and often mistaken for twins), their connection with Danny, and their fathers as alter-egos or doppelgängers (both caretakers, both angry at their wives and ambivalent towards their children, both destined to do the Overlook's dark bidding). The confusing nature of some of these doubles—for instance, we understand Charles Grady the caretaker is likely the same man as Delbert Grady, the butler, but it is never revealed how or why—only adds to their uncanniness. Thomas Allen Nelson (1982: 197) connects the uncanny figure of the double to Robin Wood's approach to understanding horror films, where the doppelgänger reflects two sides of the same persona, normality and the Monster, where the latter threatens to rise over the former in response to repression. Here, we might understand that to be repressed sexual desire—Jack's seemingly celibate relationship with Wendy, and his encounter with the woman in the bathtub in room 237 certainly suggest so, as do Kubrick's notes on King's manuscript, pointing out: 'the missing element—SEX!' (SK/15/1/2: 392). Kubrick's obsession with sex, and the conflation of sex with danger or darkness, is of course prevalent in some of his other work, notably *Lolita* and *Eyes Wide Shut*.

Given that the uncanny relies on a feeling of things being familiar, as viewers we need to believe in what we see, regardless of the perspective from which we view it. Whether we think the Overlook is haunted and Jack possessed, or see spirits like Lloyd and the Grady girls as products of the imaginations of a troubled man and his abused son, *The Shining* requires our acceptance of its phenomena to function. Kubrick achieves this by denying neat explanations or clear resolution, which has inspired countless attempts to uncover the film's 'true meaning'—a futile task by the filmmaker's own admission: 'a story of the supernatural cannot be taken apart and analysed too closely. The ultimate test of its rationale is whether it is good enough to raise the hairs on the back of your neck. If you submit it to a completely logical and detailed analysis it will eventually appear absurd'. For Kubrick, then, *The Shining* is absolutely a ghost story, one which offers 'unconscious appeal [in its] promise of immortality. If you can be frightened by a ghost story, then you must accept the possibility that supernatural beings exist. If they do, then there is more than just oblivion waiting beyond the grave' (in Ciment 1980: 475). Kubrick's notes on King's manuscript are full of rejections of exposition: 'Should he say this? Know this? Do we want such an explanation? I don't think so!' (SK/15/1/2: 371); 'We don't have to say this' (382); 'don't explain' (392); 'I don't think we should ever know what they want' (405, discussing Grady); 'silly. Silly. Don't explain. Don't explain. Idiotic. This is dumb' (406). The story's horror largely exists in showing us these impossible supernatural beings, misleading us to believe that they are inventions of the subconscious, before revealing them as absolutely real but denying any explanation. Magistrale (2003: 89) and Wright (2011: 185) notice that Jack is positioned in front of a mirror during his conversations with Lloyd and his first with Grady, so that he could be talking to himself. This seems a deliberate choice in keeping with the supernatural-psychological divide, particularly as King's novel is explicit about Jack not having the same opportunity to talk to his own reflection; his meeting with Grady takes place in the middle of the crowded ballroom, rather than its empty, mirrored bathroom, and there is no mirror behind Lloyd:

> The place was empty...but the bar was fully stocked. God be praised! Glass and silver edging on labels glowed warmly in the dark. Once, he remembered, a very long time ago, he had been angry that there was no backbar mirror. Now he was glad. Looking into it he would have seen just another drunk, fresh off the wagon: bloody nose, untucked shirt, hair rumpled, cheeks stubbly. (King 1977: 393)

At the end of the film, we are left knowing the Overlook is definitely haunted (Wendy, who is not supernaturally suggestive like her son and husband, eventually sees apparitions, and more importantly, Grady physically intervenes) but not truly understanding the connection between the hotel and Jack. Kubrick is prompting an uncanny response by asking his audience to believe the unbelievable:

> I like the regions of fantasy where reason is used primarily to undermine incredulity. Reason can take you to the border of these areas, but from there on you can be guided only by your imagination. I think we strain at the limits of reason and enjoy the temporary sense of freedom which we gain by such exercises of our imagination. (in Ciment 1980: 495-496)

The Shining presents the very human evil of Jack-as-murderer alongside Wendy's and Danny's entirely rational fear of his violence, but combines it with the supernatural suggestion of Jack-as-possessed in a haunted hotel, a balance between explanation and acceptance which is a staple of the Gothic tradition (Wright 2011: 186). It is not until Grady steps in to unlock the store cupboard that the existence of the supernatural is confirmed, and it becomes apparent that Jack has not been talking to himself all along. The narrative to this point offers a horrifying appeal to the subjective unconscious—we can be scared of a potentially violent father/husband figure, or of the Overlook's many ghosts, and Kubrick does not insist we choose. Those who see the film as losing its way once Grady manifests perhaps do not find its horror in its potential as a ghost story, but as a study of the violence of men. Understood in this way, the rejection of rational explanation and acceptance of the supernatural, confirmed by the final shot of Jack at the Overlook in 1921—whether an uncanny double, an earlier incarnation, or proof of his eternal role as caretaker—is likely infuriating. The uncertainty maintained right up to this point, however, heightens the film's uncanniness and thus its psychological effect. For Kubrick, this was the ultimate function of horror: 'Freud said that the uncanny is the only feeling which is more powerfully experienced in art than in life. If the [horror] genre required any justification, I should think this alone would serve as its credentials' (in Ciment 1980: 490).

Kubrickian style

The horror genre is comprised of a vast and ever-evolving number of cycles and subgenres which rely on an array of tropes and conventions and vary in themes and style; its overlapping categories work in conjunction with subjective effect (personal definitions of 'frightening' concepts) to make any simple and singular definition of horror difficult (Cherry 2009: 3). Over the previous decade, its biggest successes were found across an aesthetic spectrum, from the grainy, verité style of *The Texas Chain Saw Massacre* (Hooper, 1974) to the slick new horror-blockbuster feel of *The Exorcist*. *The Shining*, while arguably more closely related to the polished nature of the latter, and sharing thematic similarities with a number of previously released films, does not really look very much like a horror film—or rather, it did not look very much like mainstream audiences might have expected a major horror film to look at that point. *The Shining* is—for the most part—very brightly lit and colourful, making use of an enormous, elaborate and richly detailed set, shown off by symmetrical framing in wide angle. It features flawless tracking shots from unusual angles, many enabled by the use of the Steadicam, which Kubrick was keen to utilise as much as possible (Lightman 1980). The end result suggests a scale and artistic indulgence not often afforded to those working within a genre renowned for cheap, fast production, and the film eschews many of the conventions these low budgets were seen to lend themselves to—dark shadowy rooms, schlocky effects and cheap scares—even while utilising familiar horror iconography (blood, rotten flesh, skeletons). While *The Shining*'s visual style might have suggested to some that Kubrick did not really understand the genre he was working in, we can instead consider how elements of the *mise-en-scène* and cinematography further add to its effectiveness as a horror film. 'Kubrickian' techniques seen throughout the director's work feature prominently, and these auteurist touches are employed in ways which code meaning, enhance shock, or prolong dreadful suspense.

The film features a number of significant uses of the tracking shot. Just as these are used elsewhere in Kubrick's work, to emphasise isolation (and an impressive set) in *2001: A Space Odyssey* by following Poole (Gary Lockwood) as he jogs around Discovery One, or heighten the paranoia of *Eyes Wide Shut* by stalking Hartford (Tom Cruise) through the Manhattan streets at night, so too are they employed to set a particular mood in *The Shining*. The famous opening aerial shot tracks Jack's yellow Volkswagen Beetle as he makes his way to the Overlook for his interview, the car often just a speck as it follows the winding roads, passing cars going in the opposite direction, swamped by forest and then increasingly snow-capped mountains as the altitude increases. Although Jack assures Ullman that the trip was fine and he made it in three and a half hours ('Very good time!', Ullman responds) the sequence demonstrates just how cut off from civilisation the hotel will be once it closes for the winter, and, matched to a portentous score (an effective quotation of 'Dies Irae'), suggests the horror to come.[4] Later, Danny rides his tricycle through the hotel's corridors while the camera follows only inches from the floor, turning with the trike as he navigates his way through the maze of hallways, disorienting us just as it will later, at the end of the film, when it again tracks the boy, this time as he runs through the snow-filled hedge maze to trick and trap his father.

The most effective use of tracking comes in the sequence where Danny encounters the Grady girls. Smart editing provides the biggest effect at the end of this scene—the quick cuts between the girls standing at the end of the corridor, Danny's horrified face in close-up and back to the girls, as he 'shines' them dead and bloodied on the floor, asking him to 'Come and play with us, Danny...forever, and ever, and ever'. But the tracking shots which pre-empt his discovery cue suspense so that the tension is already heightened before he meets the girls. We have followed Danny's tricycle in earlier scenes, low to the floor and positioned very close to the boy, exploring the hotel with him. This time, however, as Danny rides through the back corridors of the kitchen, he is some way from the camera as it follows him slowly and from a slightly higher angle. Danny reaches the end of the hallway and turns, disappearing from shot although his trike can still be head in the distance. For a few seconds before we are realigned with Danny, this time back in the foreground of the frame before he turns and sees the girls, the camera continues to move forward slowly along the empty corridor. This makes it appear as if we are following Danny and something terrible is coming, at him, from behind him and aligned with the viewer's perspective—similar to the point of view shots of slasher films, for example. We do not expect Danny to happen upon the shock, we expect it to happen to him, and for us to be complicit in it.

5 Come and play with us, Danny...

This is not the only time perspective is played with in the film and the audience is aligned with the hotel's violent or supernatural forces. Consider Jack addressing us as Lloyd in the bar, before glancing at the camera from a different angle and thus reminding us of our place as entertained audience. A further example can be seen when Wendy finds Jack's manuscript, a pile of papers with 'All work and no play makes Jack a dull boy' typed over and over. After focusing on Wendy's horrified reaction, there is a cut, and she is now seen from behind, at a distance and with a wall blocking most of the view. The camera dollies left, slowly emerging from behind the wall, to find her panicked and flicking through the pages, and we watch, expecting to start moving towards toward her. Instead, and without any cut, the back of Jack's head slips in to the shot from the left, and he asks, 'How do you like it?', startling her. The result is confusing because, familiar with convention, the camera movement leads us to expect we are directly aligned with the perspective of whoever is watching Wendy. Again, we are reminded of our position as viewers, and again our discomfort is prompted by denying the realisation of that conventional expectation.

Shots common to Kubrick's work, as well as camera movement, add to the unsettling nature of *The Shining*. Jack's face in static close up, head tilted, eyes raised, bullish and threatening as he stares in to the middle-distance recalls Alex (Malcolm McDowell) in *A Clockwork Orange* and pre-empts Vincent D'Onofrio's arguably even more menacing version as Pyle (*Full Metal Jacket*). Symmetry within the frame, meanwhile, draws attention not only to its contents and their meticulous design, but also enhances the mirroring and doubling which play a significant part in the film's uncanny nature. Often, this is achieved through the use of one-point perspective, drawing the eye to the centre of the shot and the furthest distance, a common technique in Kubrick's films. This works especially well in emphasising the grandness of The Overlook's open spaces, but also enhances the hotel's ominous long hallways, and the suggestion of the potentially sinister things lurking at their ends and around their corners.

6 *Drawing us in to room 237*

Pattern and colour are also significant in creating the film's visual effect. The migraine-inducing carpets of room 237 and the hallway outside it recall the hedge maze and its confusing symmetry, but replace its natural, perennial green with vibrant clashing colours—red, orange and brown hexagons in the hallway, and a sickly green and purple pattern in the bedroom which borders on phallic; Kubrick's own notes ponder the idea of a hypnotic, Escher-esque carpet (SK15/1/3: 99). These patterns simultaneously connect and juxtapose the natural and recurring with a synthetic, striking 1970s style, emulating the tensions between past and present and the threat of repetition key to the film's themes. The bright lighting, much of which was wired in to the set as practical lighting (like the fluorescent tubes in the corridors and the grand chandeliers in the Colorado lounge and Gold Room) or provided by enormous flood lamps behind the windows of the lounge to emulate daylight, highlighted intentionally hard contrasts and vivid colours (Lightman 1980). Kubrick's dramatic use of colour can be read as symbolic—red obviously signifying death or danger (the elevator doors which gush waves of crimson blood, the bright red bathroom where Grady informs Jack that he has 'always been' the Overlook's caretaker, the bloody mess of the dead girls), blue emphasising the coldness of the Torrances' interactions or the snowy exteriors, gold associated with the wealth of past guests. But even if we ignore these possible meanings (acknowledging that all three Torrances are frequently seen wearing red and blue combined), the contrasting colours, as with many of Kubrick's other visual touches contribute to the 'uncanny' nature of the film and its unsettling effect.

***

The Shining is a clear example of Kubrick's status as 'an artist of complex and popular work' (Falsetto 1996: 18)—rather than being exclusively one or the other. Many approaches to understanding the film see it as a 'serious' work by a master filmmaker operating without commercial imperative, or elevated above a disreputable genre. This overlooks a number of important contextual considerations, not least the fact that Kubrick had been clear in asserting that he wanted to make a supernatural film, and liked a number of horror films, including *The Exorcist* and *Rosemary's Baby*—which Kubrick considered 'one of the best of the genre' (in Ciment 1980: 499). Warner Bros. had sent him King's bestseller, a novel which spoke to Kubrick's interests but also had commercial potential. *The Exorcist* had demonstrated the blockbuster appeal of horror only a few years prior, as the biggest domestic box-office draw of 1973 (Schauer and Bordwell 2006: 207) and horror production spiked at the turn of the decade when the film was released—from 35 films in 1979, to 70 in 1980 and 93 in 1981 (Prince 2002: 298). The combination of Stanley Kubrick and Stephen King promised a wide, guaranteed audience made up of dedicated fans of horror, of King's books, and of Kubrick's work, bringing genre audiences together with those of Kubrick's broad popular/arthouse appeal.

Furthermore, Kubrick, whose films 'repeatedly mix the grotesque and the banal, the conventions of Gothic confessional morbidity [...] and the self-conscious involutions of modernist parody' (Nelson 1982: 197), was ideally placed to make a horror film. His auteurist style—the use of black comedy, his artistic approach to *mise-en-scène* and cinematography, an interest in the uncanny—all lend themselves to the genre. Rather than not understanding the horror genre, or refusing to play by its rules, Kubrick instead takes its conventions, stretches and twists them, and plays with audience expectations of them. *The Shining* does not simply function as a horror film, nor is it crassly parodying one—rather, it functions as an exercise in true horror by denying our expectations, and by asking us to confront things which cannot be explained (Grady opening the store room door—a truly terrifying suggestion of the reality of the supernatural) as well as those that can (Jack's misogyny and violence):

> Kubrick systematically undermines horror tropes in *The Shining* to show the failure of cinematic forms of representation in conveying evil [...] Kubrick shows us the events on the other side of the door because he wants us to see them. Rather than this being the sign of a horror amateur who does not know how to generate cheap frights in his audience, Kubrick is repeatedly giving us the generic elements of a horror film but denying us the cathartic pleasure of a genre picture. (Browning 2009: 200)

While I agree that Kubrick takes the standard tropes of horror and asks us to confront the possibility of their reality, I disagree that *The Shining* is just a film about horror films, and with Browning's further suggestion that it is not even 'trying to be' one (211). Kubrick talked about wanting to make a horror film and that is exactly what *The Shining* is. A film made by an auteur can still be categorised within genres, even when it changes the shape of that category; contributing to a genre's evolution does not render a film outside of (or above) that genre. If *The Shining* is in many ways typical of Kubrick's style, then it surely follows that Kubrick's style was ideal for horror.

FOOTNOTES

3. More recent studies have begun to dispel (or at least destabilise) these narratives. See McAvoy (2015c), for example.
4. See Gengaro (2013) for a detailed discussion of the use of music in *The Shining*.

Chapter 2: Adapting *The Shining*

As an adaptation of a bestselling novel by an author whose popularity has grown since its publication, it is unsurprising that *The Shining* has received much attention based on its connection to King's book, especially as the reputation of both has continued to swell. Kubrick was no stranger to adaptation, and eleven of his thirteen features—from *The Killing* to *Eyes Wide Shut*—were adapted from novels or short stories (acknowledged or otherwise). Just as *The Shining* contains thematic, stylistic and tonal elements which exist elsewhere in Kubrick's films, so too can we include adaptation as a significant feature of his work, and explore how his approaches to adaptation lend themselves to horror storytelling. By examining some of the processes of adapting King's book, and by considering the reasons for additions, omissions and deviations, we can begin to establish how the film asserts its own identity within the genre, contributing an effective horror text in its own right rather than taking second place to the novel.

Kubrick opted to collaborate with Diane Johnson, an author and scholar of Gothic literature, after reading her novel *The Shadow Knows* (1974) while searching for an adaptable horror story. Ultimately selecting *The Shining*, but recognising what Johnson could bring to the project, he invited her to work on the script with him. Johnson recommended further Gothic works, and the pair discussed Freudian theory, male preoccupations with sex and death, and horror films, before they set to taking apart King's story and rebuilding it in a form to suit the screen and the filmmaker's style (Johnson 2006: 58-59). In interviews, Kubrick was often forthcoming about his broader approaches to adapting the work of others. He placed emphasis on 'flesh and feeling' over words—especially when those words would have been 'quite apparent in the situation' (Kubrick quoted in Jenkins 1997: 24), and considered the 'perfect' novel for film adaptation one focused on the 'inner life of its characters', as opposed to explicit action, which matched his abstruse style of storytelling:

> [the novel] will give the adaptor an absolute compass bearing, as it were, on what a character is thinking or feeling at any given moment of the story. And from this he can invent action which will be an objective content, will accurately dramatise this in an implicit, off-the-nose way without resorting to having the actors deliver literal statements of meaning. (Kubrick quoted in Allen 2015: 362)

When adapting *The Shining*, Kubrick, with Johnson, similarly sought to rewrite much of King's action, and to develop the characters accordingly—not just to show their thoughts and feelings, but to have this behaviour drive the drama. The starting point for writing the screenplay was to pare back King's story to its essential elements:

> The novel is by no means a serious literary work, but the plot is for the most part extremely well worked out, and for a film that is often all that really matters. With *The Shining*, the problem was to extract the essential plot and to re-invent the sections of the story that were weak. The characters needed to be developed a bit differently than they were in the novel […] [The book's] virtues lay almost entirely in the plot, and it didn't prove to be very much of a problem to adapt it in to screenplay form. (Kubrick quoted in Webster 2011: 91)

The bones of the novel's plot are retained, but Kubrick and Johnson fleshed them out with ideas of their own, removing a number of King's motifs, stripping the backstory down to vague suggestions and mentions of historical events, and significantly altering the characters, their development and relationships. Of course, this is a necessary step in translating a work of fiction from page to screen; the average novel must be compressed in order to fit a screenplay suitable for the running time of a feature-length film. But, as Jarrell D. Wright asserts in his analysis of *The Shining*'s adaptation, 'the fact that narrative compression is necessary does not illuminate the question of why a filmmaker chooses to compress one aspect of the story rather than another' (2011: 178). Rather than looking simply at *what* changes are made during an adaptation process, it is more valuable to consider *why*. In the case of *The Shining*, this can further demonstrate how Kubrick's film contributes to the horror genre. By choosing not to take forward a number of ideas central to King's book, and instead developing characters and adding scenes and motifs not featured in the novel, Kubrick made the project his own and wisely steered away from narrative threads and tropes more effectively described in words than they might be put on screen.

KING AND KUBRICK

Stanley Kubrick drew from his own interests and ideas when adapting Stephen King's novel, and eschewed a number of the central motifs within the book—much to its author's chagrin. Despite King's 'great expectations' for the adaptation, he was 'deeply disappointed with the end result'. He expressed his disdain in his 1981 book *Danse Macabre*, and followed up in a 1983 interview for *Playboy*:

> Parts of the film are chilling, charged with a relentlessly claustrophobic terror, but others fall flat. I think there are two basic problems with the movie. First, Kubrick is a very cold man—pragmatic and rational—and he had great difficulty conceiving, even academically, of a supernatural world [...] a visceral sceptic such as Kubrick just couldn't grasp the sheer inhuman evil of the Overlook Hotel. So he looked, instead, for evil in the characters, and made the film into a domestic tragedy with only vaguely supernatural overtones. That was the basic flaw: Because he couldn't believe, he couldn't make the film believable to others.
>
> The second problem was in characterization and casting. Jack Nicholson, though a fine actor, was all wrong for the part. His last big role had been in *One Flew Over The Cuckoo's Nest*, and between that and his manic grin, the audience automatically identified him as a loony from the first scene [...] If the guy is nuts to begin with, then the entire tragedy of his downfall is wasted. For that reason, the film has no center and no heart, despite its brilliantly unnerving camera angles and dazzling use of the Steadicam. What's basically wrong with Kubrick's version of *The Shining* is that it's a film by a man who thinks too much and feels too little, and that's why, for all its virtuoso effects, it never gets you by the throat and hangs on the way real horror should. (King in Norden 1983)

King saw the film as a cold exercise in stylistic posturing, a 'big, beautiful Cadillac with no engine inside it' (in Fleming Jr. 2016) which failed to grasp the basics of the genre and the nuanced character development of his book. He found its shortcomings significant enough to quickly suggest that he should like to make a corrective remake someday, 'if anybody will give me enough rope to hang myself with' (in Norden 1983)—his words prophetic, given the poor response to the eventual TV miniseries written by King and directed by Mick Garris (ABC, 1997).[5] King's complaints have been repeated over the years as the reputation of Kubrick's film grew, recently adding what he perceived as Kubrick's misogyny in reducing Wendy to a helpless, 'screaming dishrag' to his litany of issues (in Greene 2014), and taking a further swipe at Kubrick in the author's notes for his sequel to *The Shining*, *Doctor Sleep*: '[…] there was Stanley Kubrick's movie, which many seem to remember—for reasons I have never quite understood—as one of the scariest films they have ever seen….[The novel is the] True History of the Torrance Family' (King 2013: 483). King was, it seems, perplexed and dismayed by the filmmaker's persistence in doing things his own way. Despite discussing the project with Kubrick during pre-production, his ideas were ultimately not required:

> My single conversation with the late Stanley Kubrick, about six months before he commenced filming on his version of *The Shining*, suggested that it was [the blurred line between the supernatural and psychotic] that appealed to him: what, exactly, is impelling Jack Torrance toward murder in the winter-isolated rooms and hallways of the Overlook Hotel? Is it undead people, or undead memories? Mr. Kubrick and I came to different conclusions (I always thought there were malevolent ghosts in The Overlook, driving Jack to the precipice), but perhaps those different conclusions are, in fact, the same. For aren't memories the true ghosts of our lives? Do they not drive all of us to words and acts we regret from time to time? (King 2001, in 2011: xii)

King's assertion that Kubrick did not grasp the supernatural horror of *The Shining* echo a number of critical responses, but ultimately suggest a failure to engage with the uncanny and ambiguous nature of the film's themes. Kubrick's ghosts are intentionally configured so that a viewer can choose to understand them as either Jack's alternative personalities, or manifestations of past Overlook residents. This offers verisimilitude for even the most sceptical viewers, ensuring that, by the time Grady unlocks the pantry door, we are horrified to discover the ghosts are entirely real. The initial ambiguity renders the question of what is driving Jack toward murder unanswerable for much of the film's narrative—but Kubrick's conclusion is not as far from King's as the author insists; Jack, regardless of issues which exist before he arrives at the hotel, is clearly haunted, driven 'to the precipice' by Lloyd, Grady, and the Overlook itself. The suggestion that Kubrick avoided the supernatural because he did not believe in it further ignores his open interest in the subject—made as clear in King's and Kubrick's discussions as in the director's admissions elsewhere.

There are some contradictions in King's complaints. In 1983, he told *Playboy* of 'transatlantic calls to me at odd hours of the night and day' (in Norden 1983), and mentioned a set visit to meet Kubrick in a BBC interview (2013)—but in the foreword to a new edition of *The Shining* in 2001, quoted above, he claims he had a 'single conversation' with the filmmaker. He has stated that the first time he saw the film, he 'didn't care for it much' (in Fleming Jr. 2016), but notes, understandably: 'I had to keep my mouth shut at the time. It was a screening, and Nicholson was there' (in Greene 2014). Memos between Warner Bros. executives held in the Stanley Kubrick archives confirm arrangements for a private, pre-press screening for King in New York on 21st May 1980, two days before the film's initial release, and subsequently report King's reaction to the film:

> As you know, Stephen King screened the picture yesterday and loved it…perhaps George Nelson [Warner Bros.] could double check with Kirby McCauley [King's then-agent] just to make sure that King's reaction was as genuine as it seemed to be, in favour of the picture. (Julian Senior, 1980, Memo to Rob Friedman 'RE. Stephen King', May 22. WB FeaPub 0151 Shining #3, SK/15/5/2/4)

At the bottom of this is a handwritten note, presumably made during a check with McCauley: 'positive, masterpiece with flaws faithful to the book', which is confirmed in a responding memo:

> [McCauley] assures that Stephen King truly had positive reaction. Considered film faithful to book, and, in any interview, will say good things to promote the film. (George Nelson, 1980, Memo to Julian Senior 'RE. Stephen King', May 22. WB FeaPub 0151 Shining #3, SK/15/5/2/4)

It is of course plausible that these discussions were veiled in the public relations spin of literary agents and advertising executives, that Warner Bros., in wanting King on-record and on-side for the release, emphasised his polite positivity over his identification of the film's 'flaws', or that King felt compelled at such a late stage to praise, rather than critique, Kubrick's work. The memos, however, suggest an immediate response quite different to King's not 'caring for it much', and it appears as though his dislike of the film grew over the years after it came out. Some theories speculate that King's reaction can be attributed in part to the book's autobiographical theme—not uncommon for King's work, but *The Shining*, written shortly before King realised his own alcoholism, seems particularly personal (Greene 2014). At least as likely is that *The Shining* was one of the more notable adaptations of King's work, by a major filmmaker guaranteed to attract attention, and he was continually asked to comment on it as its reputation grew. With the exception of *Carrie*, which he considered 'fantastic' (in Norden 2012), the author has been rather ambivalent about most other filmed versions of his work:

> The movies have never been a big deal to me. The movies are the movies. They just make them. If they're good, that's terrific. If they're not, they're not. But I see them as a lesser medium than fiction, than literature, and a more ephemeral medium. (in Greene 2014)

This argument, and the question King is responding to—if it is possible that Kubrick 'made a great movie that just so happens to be a horrible adaptation of your book?'— highlight a major problem with understanding adaptation; that the film can never be considered on its own merits if fidelity is used as a benchmark for success: 'King appears to have been under the persistent misapprehension that Kubrick wanted to make a faithful adaptation of his novel; King appears to have consistently failed to grasp that this was never Kubrick's intention' (Webster 2011: 92). Faithfulness to a written source is neither necessary nor always possible in adaptation, but its lack no doubt stings the author of not only successful, but deeply personal, work.

PREFATORY MATTERS

The most obvious change made in *The Shining*'s adaptation is that the screenplay 'clears out the clutter' of the novel's bloated backstory (Luckhurst 2013: 38-39), allowing a more immediate introduction to the family's isolation, and enabling Kubrick's favoured 'slow start, the start that goes under the audience's skin and involves them so that they can appreciate grace notes and soft tones and don't have to be pounded over the head with plot points and suspense hooks' (quoted in Nelson 1982: 10). King's narrative drifts back and forth in time, using characters' memories to provide motivation for action which unfolds in the present. These include the history of Jack's childhood with his own abusive father, lengthy chapters which offer detailed accounts of previous violent episodes—the drunken assault on Danny, and an attack on a seventeen-year-old student, George Hatfield, which leaves the boy concussed and costs Jack his prep school job—and a series of incidents and conversations with Jack's colleague and drinking buddy Al Shockley. There are also countless reflections from the perspectives of all three Torrances on Jack and Wendy's strained marriage (Danny shines his parents thinking about divorce—a trick Kubrick found 'corny' [SK/15/1/3: 28-29]), Jack recalls cruel verbal attacks on his wife, Wendy romantically mourns the couple's happier years). Placing these recollections in early chapters portends the horrible repetition of history so central to *The Shining*'s narrative; Jack struggles with his feelings about his father but is inclined to addiction and abuse in just the same way (even repeating his threatening 'come here and take your medicine' line to both Hatfield [King 1977: 124], and later at the Overlook to Danny [463]), just as he will inevitably become the hotel's new murderous caretaker. Rather than include these details as a prologue, or clumsy flashback, in the film we instead learn about Jack's drinking, and how he broke Danny's arm, through a conversation between Wendy and a doctor (or in the initial UK cut, during Jack's first meeting with Lloyd). King uses Jack's family history as an explanation for his behaviour (just as in *Doctor Sleep* Danny, as an adult, faces his own addiction problems), but condensing this into the screenplay would risk a hackneyed, heavy-handed explanation.

Kubrick's and Johnson's notes on King's manuscript evidence the stripping away of exposition in the early stages of adaptation, particularly in the first part of the book, tellingly titled 'Prefatory Matters'. Against a long sequence where Shockley and Jack drunkenly run their car over a child's bike late one night (no body is found, but the event haunts Jack and triggers his sobriety), a handwritten question: 'Do we need this? A good scene but what is the point?' (SK/15/1/3: 41-42), and later: 'the story lags. Too much attempt to build character' (48), 'v. little plot in this chapter' (58). Sixty pages of the novel are automatically dispensed with, and just two main scenes saved: Jack's interview, and a sequence with Wendy and a psychiatrist, to introduce characters and plot before cutting to the family on their journey to the Overlook for closing day. These were later expanded to include lunch between Danny and Wendy at home, where Danny's 'imaginary friend' Tony ('a little boy who lives in my mouth', who appears to control the boy's shining; Danny animates him by waggling his finger and dropping his voice to a childish growl) makes it clear that he does not want the family to go to the Overlook; a short phone call from Jack at the hotel to tell Wendy he got the job; and Danny's first vision—the elevator spewing blood, a brief glimpse of the Grady girls, and Danny screaming silently. By changing the psychiatrist to a doctor, Danny's gift is kept unexplained until his later meeting with Halloran. Within the film's first scenes, then, we are introduced to the Torrances and the Overlook, told that Danny has some kind of psychic ability, and have anticipated the hotel's horrors through a gruesome, expressionist montage which gives little away. Comparing these early parts of the story demonstrates the way in which Kubrick's economy with narrative emphasises the variable options for interpretation: 'Kubrick speeds his project, but whittles down the fullness of King's story. Transformed, it is already becoming elliptical, mysterious' (Jenkins 1997: 77). By not cutting back and forth in time, and by putting the Torrances alone at the Overlook much sooner (a fifth of King's book passes before the family shut the door on Ullman for the winter), the sense of isolation is also amplified. Details of the Overlook's past are also discarded. In the novel, Jack finds an enormous scrapbook of news clippings about past guests, murders, suicides and accidents at the hotel, which are covered by King in extensively detailed stories (1977: 167-182). Scenes with the scrapbook were filmed (the prop, a fascinatingly thorough and aged collection of gruesome clippings, can be found in the Kubrick archives), but deemed unnecessary and ultimately excluded for length. Diane Johnson has expressed disappointment with the cut: 'Without the scene, which explains Jack's transition from depressed and blocked writer to one suddenly filled with (demonic) energy, writing at great speed and piling high the pages of manuscript, his change seems abrupt and unmotivated' (2006: 58). Johnson is right in that the shift seems sudden, but the lack of explicit motivation for this change speaks to Kubrick's tendency for only the vaguest explanations.

The novel features two motifs left out of the adaptation, which provide impetus for a number of events and offer some rather heavy-handed symbolism. Jack comes across a wasps' nest while retiling the hotel's roof, empties it with a bug bomb and gives it to Danny as a present, only for the wasps to return and attack the family in the middle of the night. This provides a metaphor for the recurrence of horrible events (Jack's own father gave him a similar gift as a child) and prompts Jack's recollection of repressed memories. It also suggests that the most dangerous creatures are not, like bees, those who attack once and die, but wasps who, like Jack, are prone to sting over and over if prompted, because it is simply their nature.[6] The wasps' nest's meaning is spelled out to the reader: 'it seemed to [Jack] that it could serve as both a workable symbol for what he had been through (and what he had dragged his hostages to fortune through) and an omen for a better future' (King 1977: 117); 'You could be stung, but you could also sting back' (125). The second discarded motif is the old, temperamental boiler which heats the Overlook and has to be maintained as part of Jack's caretaker role. This is a more immediate warning of danger—it has to be decompressed daily to avoid the machine exploding and burning down the hotel. As Jack's madness rises, so does the boiler's pressure, eventually blowing, killing Jack in the middle of his murderous rampage and destroying the Overlook as Wendy and Danny escape with Halloran. These symbols of violent pasts and repressed rage were omitted from the film, Kubrick noting the wasps were 'dispensable' and 'such an effort' (SK/15/1/3: 146-148), and, perhaps in anticipation of the difficulty filming a convincing, large scale destruction of the hotel, or otherwise just rejecting its clunky metaphor: 'fuck the boiler' (SK/15/1/2: 382).

In its place, the frozen hedge maze functions as the means of Jack's demise. As Jarrell D. Wright notes, the maze—absent from the novel—is often connected to the topiary animals guarding the front lawn of King's Overlook, which come to life and attack Danny, Jack and Halloran in separate incidents, but their only real similarity is as ornamental garden features, and the maze is more accurately equated with the boiler (2011: 179). King's comparison of the fire and ice endings of both stories is apt in this regard, but we can understand the maze's function somewhere between the two interpretations. It replaces the boiler and removes the need for the other outside spaces of the book (the topiary animals, a playground and a roque court). It simplifies the vast grounds of the hotel (much in the same way the narrative clutter of the novel is reduced) while emphasising its scale and grandeur, and provides a visually pleasing pattern in keeping with Kubrick's style. It is also a continuation of the uncanny doubling at play throughout the film, reflecting both the hotel's claustrophobic, labyrinthine hallways and the miniature model maze which Jack hulks over as Danny and Wendy navigate the full scale version, and it speaks to connections with myths and fairy tales (the minotaur in the labyrinth, and the 'trail of breadcrumbs' which Wendy references earlier when commenting how the hotel feels like a maze. Danny later traces his own footsteps in the snow when escaping the maze, just like a trail of breadcrumbs). Furthermore, in its false turns and dead ends, it reflects the growing confusion and mystery of the film.[7] Removing the boiler's obvious metaphorical theme of rising pressure, the film's elliptical narrative instead works much more subtly to increase the tension, gradually compressing the passing of time, the temporal spaces between events, which are marked by intertitles reducing from 'a month later', to days, then hours ('Saturday', 'Monday', 'Wednesday', '8am', '4pm') (Nelson 1982: 231). The novel uses a similar approach at the beginning of its later chapters to signpost developing events at the Overlook and Halloran's journey, running parallel: 'at 8.31 a.m., MST…' (King 1977: 395), 'Around noon' (402), 'It was three in the afternoon of a long, long day' (410), 'It was quarter of two in the afternoon' (426), but the orderly progression of the film's events once the family are alone (every other day, then divisible hours) is in keeping with the film's use of patterns and the ordered presentation of disorderly events.

7 Jacks keeps an eye on his family

THE (UN)DENIABLE SUPERNATURAL

A number of the book's key frightening episodes are removed or reimagined to maintain (for as long as possible) the option that the hauntings are figments of Jack's imagination. The hedge animals' attacks are among the most effective sections of King's story, as horrifying as any of the Overlook's ghosts as they change position (heard and felt, but not seen) behind Jack's and Danny's backs, getting closer before eventually pouncing. It is certainly plausible that Kubrick could have developed a workable scene with the creatures, but as with the wasps' nest, they were dismissed in adaptation as 'an effort' (SK/15/1/3: 148)—a wise decision, if the poor effect of the equivalent scene in King and Garris's miniseries offers a fair indication of the end result. The television re-adaptation, unsurprisingly much more faithful to King's novel, reinstates a few motifs rejected by Kubrick and Johnson, including the topiary creatures, the wasps' nest, a snake-like fire hose that comes to life and attacks Danny, and an automaton clock with axe-wielding characters (replacing the figures of King's book which, on one occasion, perform sex acts as the clock chimes, and on another club a boy to death), and a clock face that gives way to a black hole, triggering Danny's visions. While it is unfair to directly compare the series with Kubrick's film in terms of quality (contrasts in budgets, format and audience ensure differences between the two, as does the near twenty year gap in production and their very different writers), the execution of these scenes suggest they are events possibly better suited to written words and readers' imaginations than they are realised on screen. Looking at differences in the realisation of scenes, however, does offer insight regarding the effectiveness of Kubrick's and Johnson's adaptation choices.

The figure of the dogman provides an interesting point of comparison between book, film and television. In the novel, he is identified as Roger, the lover of Horace Derwent, a former owner of the Overlook who Jack meets at a ghostly costume party in the Gold Room. A fellow partygoer tells Jack that Horace is stringing Roger along, making him dress and act as a pet dog for his amusement. Earlier, Danny encounters the man in the hallway, dressed in a sparkly dog suit minus his mask, drenched in sweat, smeared with blood and stinking of scotch. He barks and growls at Danny, and threatens him when the boy asks to be let by: 'Not by the hair on my chinny-chin-chin [...] I'm going to eat you up, little boy. And I think I'll start with your plump little *cock*', before calling after his partner: 'Get it up, Harry you bitch-bastard! [...] I'll *huff*...and I'll *puff*...until Harry Derwent's *all bloowwwwn down!*' (King 1977: 369). Kubrick's film shows who we presume to be Roger and Harry for just a single shot, caught in the middle of this act by Wendy as she tries to escape the Overlook. This retains the sexual elements of the scene, the man's face obscured by his mask and his costume changed from a silver to a brown fur, making him more animal-like, closing the uncanny gap—but it denies us any explanation of the men's identities or their connection to the hotel, and viewers of the film unfamiliar with King's book would be left totally in the dark. Jack, who in early treatments was intended to be the dogman (SK/15/1/2: 391), picks up the horrible references to the big bad wolf later, as he breaks down the bathroom door with his axe. The TV series reinstates Danny's encounter in the hallway, but with a sharp-suited man in a rubber wolf head, who jumps out from a doorway and tells Danny he's going to eat him: 'I'm going to start at your toes and work my way up.' The explicit, nasty encounter of King's book does not work as effectively in this sanitised version with a cheap mask and jump scares. In the film, by replacing Danny with Wendy, Kubrick's mysterious, grotesquely sexual translation bends the scene to fit his uncanny tone, and despite its strangeness, the encounter performs a narrative function in showing Wendy that the hotel is haunted.

8 Wendy meets Harry and Roger

The reduction of more significant aspects of King's story is evident elsewhere in the adaptation, rendering whole chapters to brief, unexplained moments in keeping with the film's strangeness. Kubrick shows us ghostly evidence of, as the bloodied man Wendy encounters puts it, a 'great party', in balloons and streamers left scattered through the hallways, and the cobweb-covered skeletons sitting around champagne magnums. This can be connected to the event where Jack meets Grady, presumably the July 4th ball of 1921 that appears in the final shot's photograph. But this revelry is minimal (and late) in comparison to the novel, where the party is central in confirming Danny and Wendy's suspicions that the hotel is haunted. The pair hear sounds of music and laughter, animated chatter, corks popping, doors slamming, evidence of the Overlook 'coming to life around them' (King 1977: 419), and find confetti, party favours, bottles and masks in an elevator which runs of its own accord—replaced, of course, with Danny's shine of the double elevator which unleashes a torrent of claret blood. Kubrick's ghosts, then, are evident (at least by the end of the film—not only does Grady free Jack, but Wendy sees the dogman, party goer and skeletons, and we presume that she is not 'seeing things' in the ways Jack and Danny could be) but often not prominent; the silence and emptiness of the hotel's vast, empty corridors provides the unsettling dread for much of the film, and the overt, intrusive hauntings of the novel would likely detract from this tone, the significance of Jack's threat, and the effect of the film's most horrible sequences—the gushing blood, Danny's encounter with the Grady girls, the sequence in room 237, and Jack's final attack.

Central to the adaptation, Johnson notes (and as discussed in the previous chapter), was balance in presenting the supernatural in a rational way which avoided depending 'unduly on ghosts and gimmicks for horrific effect' while providing some level of explanation for the events through psychology, focusing on the human responses and behaviours prompted by supernatural phenomena (2006: 55-56). The realisation of the uncanny was tantamount to Kubrick's concern that 'the movie be scary'; these fine lines between reality/belief and supernatural/psychological were important to the adaptation. Johnson maintains that the Overlook's apparitions are both 'supernatural forces' and 'psychological projections' in some form or other—perhaps generated by imagination, but once created, powerful and malevolent (58). Explanation for the haunting was essential but minimal—the Native American burial ground the hotel is built on providing some rationale—but the supernatural events and occurrences could be left open to interpretation; Kubrick was comfortable with the 'paradox of something being both true and untrue at the same time' (59). This is illustrated well by the scene in room 237. The novel's equivalent room is 217, and was changed to avoid problems with future guests fearful of staying in the room at the Timberline (LoBrutto 1997: 416) (although predictably, as the hotel's website boasts, 217 is now their most commonly requested room). In the novel, Danny stands outside 217 for a long time, thinking about the Bluebeard folktale of a wealthy man who murders his wives and hides them away in a locked room. He finds a dead woman in the bath, who comes to life and attacks him. Jack visits 217 twice, finding just the woman's shadow the first time, and George Hatfield the second. There is no question that the characters have seen (and engaged with) the ghosts. In the film, Danny enters the room, but we do not see what takes place inside. Instead, he opens the door and there is an immediate cut to Wendy, hearing Jack in the midst of a nightmare. When she wakes him, he tells her it was 'the most horrible dream I ever had [...] I killed you and Danny. But I didn't just kill you. I cut you up into little pieces'. This clearly disturbs Jack, who, visibly shaken, worries, 'I must be losing my mind'. Wendy is horrified by the admission. As Danny enters the scene, his neck bruised and his jumper torn, his parents' responses change. Wendy moves from her distraught husband's side, swiftly turning her concern to Danny and becoming accusatory and angry toward Jack ('You did this to him, didn't you? You son of a bitch!'). Jack, lost for words, does not answer. But his shrug, and his expression—blankly crazy, but not defiant—suggests that he cannot truthfully answer Wendy's question; neither can the viewer. Danny later, off-screen, tells his mother that an old woman in 237 hurt him. Wendy finds Jack in the Gold Room and insists he investigate. He retorts, 'Are you out of your fucking mind?', despite being interrupted in the midst of a conversation with a phantom bartender as he drinks imaginary bourbon. On visiting the room, he does not find an old woman, but a young, nude one, in the bathtub. She rises and moves toward him, and he gladly accepts her advances; they embrace and kiss before she changes in his arms, now an aged hag with rotting flesh. He flees back to the family's room and reassures Wendy that 237 contains 'nothing at all…I didn't see one god damn thing'. Jack engages with the spirits but, maybe frightened that he is losing his mind, or otherwise not wanting his family to catch wind of the plan the hotel has for him (which he soon willingly accepts), he denies their existence. Both he and Danny are unreliable narrators. Jack's mental state (or even possession) and Danny's shining render their visions as exactly that—as viewers, we can chose to believe in the ghosts, but at this stage in the film we cannot be sure that they are anything more than the product of imagination, and Danny's injuries could feasibly be caused by his father, the woman, or—

at a stretch—himself, as Jack suggests to Wendy when he lies that he found nothing in the room. This is supported by early notes on the script treatment, in which Danny, not Jack, finds the woman in the bath, and Jack finds only a shadow: 'his fear is more than the sense of the horrible thing in the bathtub—he has a momentary perception of his own mental state' and suspects that he might have hurt his son (SK/15/1/19). He lies to Wendy for two reasons: he does not want his wife to doubt his sanity, and the hotel is influencing him (SK/15/1/3: 288). Both are plausible options, and each adds a layer of horror to the narrative.

9 Jack finds 'not a god damn thing' in room 237

JACK TORRANCE

Kubrick and Johnson felt that the story's thematic strength was connected to the broken family, and the Torrances' resentments and fears, and agreed this should take priority over the novel's preoccupations with alcoholism and ambition (Johnson in McAvoy 2015b). Similarly, in refocusing from Danny's psychic power to Jack's easily influenced psychological state, changes to characters and relationships are central to King's issues with the film and Kubrick's approach to adaptation, and are apparent from the beginning of the narrative. The novel features multiple descriptions of the three bonding, flashbacks to earlier, happier times in the Torrance family history, and moments of tenderness between Jack and his wife and son. Although the bond between Wendy and Danny is established early on, screen Jack seems to tolerate his family at best, and the family are separated for a fair amount of the film's running time. In the first scenes, this serves a convenient function, allowing Jack to visit the hotel and learn a little about its past, Danny to demonstrate his shining, and Wendy's discussion with the doctor to acquaint us with Jack's past violence. Once at the hotel, Danny spends a lot of time playing alone, meaning 'his parents seem a trifle thoughtless' (Jenkins 1997: 79), although this also emphasises the family's isolation, the boy's trike echoing in the empty hallways, the tennis ball rolling silently across the carpet. Furthermore, in keeping Jack away from his family, the influence of the hotel on him is apparent from the beginning: 'splitting Jack away from his family is necessary and good—and frightening' (SK/15/1/2: 391).

In the film, Jack seems at home at the Overlook from the moment he arrives, and he later tells Wendy that he has never been as happy or as comfortable anywhere, that he felt a sense of déjà vu on coming for his interview. Although there is nothing explicit in the opening scene that suggests he has 'always been' there, he is at least comfortable in the hotel's surroundings. We first see him strolling in to the Colorado Lounge, looking around and taking in the grand room's décor and guests, before announcing himself confidently to the receptionist, who gives him directions to Ullman's office. His introduction to the manager is convivial, the pair make small talk about Jack's journey as they settle in to the interview, which continues in a friendly fashion suggesting the meeting is nothing but a formality—Jack already has the job. Conversely, the book's Ullman makes his feelings about offering him the role clear during a tense, hostile exchange where he expresses reservations about hiring a former drunk bringing a family to the hotel. The last time that happened, the candidate was Delbert Grady, and hiring him resulted in the murder of his wife and daughters. If it were up to him, Ullman tells Jack, he would not take him on. Jack, unemployed after having been fired from his prestigious prep school job, desperately needs the caretaker role but very clearly feels it is beneath him, as he goes to pains to point out to Ullman, telling him that in hiring Grady, his mistake was selecting a man without a college education. Throughout this chapter's exchange, Jack inwardly rages, flashing a 'PR smile' that is 'large and insultingly toothy' (King, 1977: 6), clenching his fists, responding to Ullman's questions with sarcasm and repeatedly describing the manager—from the book's opening words—as an 'officious little prick' (3). Ullman is officious, as well as patronising and brusque, but still we get an idea of Jack's temperament and attitude from the very first words of King's book. He is self-important, angry, combative and responds badly to being belittled. Even at this stage, it is clear that Jack may not be the most sympathetic narrator. His early empathy for Grady, rather than the man's murdered family ('Did they scream? he wondered. Poor Grady [...] he shouldn't have been here. And he shouldn't have lost his temper' [27]), further underlines his violent inclinations.

Nicholson's Torrance is equally adept at the 'big PR smile', and the interview conveys the same information (aside from the drinking—Jack declares 'we don't drink' when Ullman shows them the unstocked Gold Room bar, but his addiction is not acknowledged in the interview as it is in King's book) but the film's equivalent scene maintains its cheerful atmosphere. Jack's confidence comes across as a genuine desire to make a good impression from a man who very much wants (rather than only needs) the job. He frames the appeal in the Overlook's isolation; working on a new writing project, being cut off from civilisation for a few months is, he says, 'exactly what I'm looking for'. Jack is 'intrigued' to learn about the Grady family's grisly demise, and says his wife, as a 'confirmed ghost story and horror film addict', will be fascinated. Given Nicholson's expressive performance, his lack of concern on hearing this horrible story cannot simply be nuanced reaction—Jack is totally on board with the hotel and its history. King's Jack hates Ullman and resents being reduced to becoming a winter caretaker. Kubrick's Jack wants in to the Overlook, and soon. He's engaged and intrigued as soon as he steps into the hotel, 'psychologically prepared to do its murderous bidding. He doesn't have very much farther to go for his anger and frustration to become completely uncontrollable' (Kubrick in Ciment 1980: 493).

Just as our introduction to Jack varies between book and film, so too does his relationship with his family, and the nature of the interviews further emphasises these contrasts. The earliest interactions between Jack and his wife and son which follow the hostile interview of King's novel are caring (Danny greets his father and tells him he loves him) or intimate (after sex, Wendy reminisces about the early days of their relationship)—even though they are interspersed with flashbacks of Jack's drinking days, breaking Danny's arm, and attacking the boy at school, or visions of horrible things to come through Danny's shining:

> Danny ran toward him and then froze, his eyes widening. His heart crawled up into the middle of his throat and froze solid. Beside his daddy, in the other front seat, was a short-handled mallet, its head clotted with blood and hair. Then it was just a bag of groceries […] He went to his daddy and buried his face in Daddy's sheepskin-lined denim jacket and hugged him tight tight tight. (King 1977: 37)

In the film, Jack's phone call to Wendy immediately following the interview is relatively perfunctory—practically exposition. The first scene which features the family all together is in the car on the way to the Overlook for the winter. Jack appears largely disinterested in his passengers, responding to questions with grunts or single word answers—but snaps at Danny, 'Well, you shoulda eaten your breakfast' when the boy complains he's hungry, and sarcastically moans to Wendy, 'You see, it's okay, he saw it on the television!' when they discuss a party who got lost in the mountains and resorted to cannibalism. His first scene alone with Wendy, when she wakes him with breakfast after he sleeps in late, begins playfully but he becomes snide, irritated when she suggests he needs to get back in to the habit of writing, and mocks her having been scared of the hotel when they first arrived. This can be ascribed to narrative economy—a convincing gradual arc from loving parent to violent patriarch harder to achieve in under three hours than on 500 pages—but more importantly, it introduces Kubrick's black humour and an unsettling, grotesque parody of family life. Complaints of Kubrick's coldness may well be justified here; the warmth of the family relationship is missing from the outset, but with good reason. Furthermore, while the good/bad Jack introductions are almost entirely switched in adaptation, Jack's instability, hostility, and grim empathy for Grady are clearly set out from the book's opening; King's suggestion that Nicholson's 'crazier than a shithouse rat' Jack (quoted in Fleming Jr. 2016) is vastly different from his literary Torrance is overemphasised. The benefit of Jack's tense exchanges with his family, rather than with Ullman, is that it anticipates the dread of Wendy and Danny (and the viewer) being trapped with this man. Ullman has nothing personal to fear of Jack's potential cabin fever, but—as I will explore further in the next chapter—his wife and child most definitely do.

'CORRECTING' DICK HALLORAN

One particularly cruel change is the demise of Dick Halloran, who is denied the hero status awarded him in the book as a surviving saviour, and in the film is instead killed by Jack the minute he arrives to rescue the family. Having the only black character in the film killed off—particularly given he survives the novel—prompted accusations of racism from some critics, to which I will return in the following chapter; it is worth first considering the reasons for the change within the context of adaptation. Danny and Dick's psychic connection through their mutual shining is pushed to full effect in the book, and Halloran's character remains much more central even after he leaves the Overlook for the winter. The pair's initial meeting is much longer, their conversations about their gift extensive, detailed and personal. The narrative repeatedly switches back to Halloran's perspective as he worries about the stranded family, and he and Danny reconnect frequently as the boy tries to telepathically call him for help. Dick returns to the Overlook, fights Jack (and the hotel's ghosts), saves Danny and Wendy, and drives them off to safety in the Snowcat. In an epilogue, Halloran has taken on an almost fatherly role, becoming the caring, supportive patriarch that Jack, even in his saner, sober moments, had never quite been—a relationship furthered in flashbacks and Danny's adult shinings in *Doctor Sleep*. Kubrick's Halloran never has this opportunity. His connection with Danny is that of a mentor, and their conversations are conducted accordingly—Danny approaches their talk about the shining with caution, keen to learn but keeping details of his abilities to himself. In the book, Danny and Halloran communicate in clearer language through their shining ('!!! OH DICK OH PLEASE PLEASE PLEASE COME !!!' [King 1977: 338]), but in keeping with Kubrick's expressionist style, Danny projects his vision of the blood flooding the elevator shaft and the pair's connection is kept symbolic.

Early in the adaptation process, Kubrick toyed with drastically changing Dick's role in the narrative. Arriving back at the hotel in response to Danny's calls, a battle between Jack and Halloran was to take place. Notes made on King's manuscript discuss how to approach this scene: 'when Halloran gets there, is there a new and cleverer wrinkle we can use for the final battle between Halloran and Jack, or should they just fight it out?' (SK15/1/1). For a while during development, variations of the script suggested Halloran as the eventual monster, and describe Danny trying to escape a 'murderous' Dick, 'by

10 Danny meets Halloran

now an appaling [sic] figure of savagery, smashing at the walls with an axe, snarling, shrieking, foaming and chocking [sic]':

> Snarling
> Grunting
> Frenzied
> Animal like
> Panting
> Foaming and chocking [sic] with frenzied rage shrieking bellowing roaring maniacally (ibid.)

But having Halloran become so overtaken by the Overlook's powerful ghosts makes little sense. If Jack, predisposed to violence and clearly impressionable, takes several weeks to give in to the hotel's murderous plot, it would not be believable to have Halloran, who has been aware of the hauntings and their horrible potential for years, succumb to them so quickly; even if his ESP is used as explanation. Danny, who shares Dick's gift, sees the ghosts on account of his ability to shine—but refuses to 'come and play' with them. We should assume the man shares the boy's strength. Halloran cannot be excluded from the narrative altogether; his character is essential to make sense of Danny's visions and to provide some context for the hotel's mysterious past. His rescue attempt also belongs in the adaptation; it is logical that the boy would reach out to him, and that Dick would respond by trying to save the Torrances (although, as Kubrick noted, it was important that the scene was not 'Clark Kent to the rescue' [SK/15/1/2: 362]). But in a story which has worked hard to configure Jack as the monster of the piece, Halloran is expendable and Wendy and Danny can save themselves. In King's novel, no-one is killed; Kubrick included the murder and changed Halloran from hero to victim as he felt strongly that a character needed to die in order to fulfil the generic requirements of a horror film. After everything that Wendy and Danny go through, it would be too cruel to see mother or son killed, and Jack, as the villain, must die: 'so after all was said and done, there was nobody but Halloran and that's why he got it' (Johnson in McAvoy 2015b: 560).

***

In responses to any adaptation, even with an understanding of the requirements of translating a story from book to film—the focus on the visual to match the cinematic form (especially significant when the internal monologue of the novel's narrators is removed), or the need to economically trim characters, subplots or motifs to fit a film's length—there is a tendency to critique a film based on its faithfulness to the source. Reception often leans toward lamenting what is lost in translation, or at least what is removed or altered, rather than what might be gained, or how the end result might be a completely different story. Comparing films with their adapted sources inevitably results in finding cinematic shortfalls; screenwriters are seen to 'miss the point', directors to focus on the 'wrong things' and in the 'wrong ways', actors are 'poorly cast' as characters that authors created and readers imagined. It is impossible to objectively watch a film adaptation of a book we love (and harder, no doubt, to view a version of something we created), because we already have a distinct look and feel for the story in our mind. By exploring the reasons for changes, and by viewing omissions, additions and deviations as neither erroneous nor 'disrespectful' but rather as the necessary result of both the change in form (book to film) and in author (King to Kubrick), we can consider the film on its own merits.

King's response to Kubrick's work is natural, given his attachment, and it matches the (often less passionate) inclination of viewers and critics who favour the book. Stanley

Kubrick's *The Shining* is not best approached as an adaptation of Stephen King's novel if the aim is to understand or appreciate the film on its own terms: 'perhaps the best approach to Kubrick's *The Shining* is to divorce it from connections with Stephen King—not because Kubrick failed to do justice to King's narrative, but simply because it has ceased to be King's' (Collings in Magistrale 2003: 96). The adaptation provides not only a more effective onscreen imagining of King's story than an ultra-faithful, page-by-page retelling would yield (as the TV series suggests), but results in a film of 'streamlined, if sometimes penumbral, simplicity' (Jenkins 1997: 87), which matches Kubrick's visual style and thematic obsessions. Looking at how and why parts of the book were adapted (rather than just focusing on what changed) allows for a coherent appreciation of Kubrick's film as a significant horror movie. Furthermore, *The Shining* provides an ideal case study for more nuanced theories of adaptation which consider films 'in relation to the history of generic conventions within which both the film and its source text are situated. In other words, a film participates in—and should therefore be conceptualized as part of—a sequence of adaptations of which the "original" text, in turn, constitutes a segment' (Wright 2011: 175). Changing the story's horrific nature does not result in it being less suited to the horror genre, it just offers a different take on its conventions. Comparing the film directly to its equally iconic source text results in inevitable competition in which the original will often 'win', even when then the two serve different functions. In addition to analysing adaptation, considering the film within the context of its production and its creators' filmmaking style, and looking at its position within the genre and its themes, offers a fuller picture of *The Shining*'s effective approach to horror.

FOOTNOTES

5. See Robinson (2013) for a detailed analysis of the series which identifies a number of the issues in striving for fidelity to the novel.
6. Graham Allen (2015) uses the metaphor of the 'unempty' wasps nest to examine the intertextual process of adaptation between the book and film, where the nest can be reconfigured in to an understanding of Kubrick's film.
7. See Nelson (1982) and Luckhurst (2013) for further detailed analyses of the maze's significance.

Chapter 3: Genre and Themes

The Shining has attracted countless analyses of its themes and explorations of its supposedly hidden meanings. Through thirty-odd years of growing critical reputation and academic consideration, alongside cult appreciation aided by re-releases and digital formats and encouraged by the spread of online fan activity, the film has garnered a reputation not only as one of the greatest horror films of the twentieth century, but as the subject of obsessive analysis and interpretation. The theories as to Kubrick's unconfirmed intentions in making *The Shining*, and the resulting 'real meaning' of his film, range from the entirely reasonable to the outlandishly conspiratorial. Rodney Ascher's 2013 documentary *Room 237* explores a number of these theories, including Bill Blakemore's observation that the film is packed with (not-so-subtle) references to the genocide of Native American peoples (the larder is stocked with Calumet baking powder, the Colorado Lounge's artwork is Native American, and Ullman explicitly states that the Overlook is 'built on an Indian burial ground') and Geoffrey Cocks's reading of *The Shining* as a Holocaust metaphor, which highlights potential allusions in the film as 'proof' of Kubrick's preoccupation with the topic (an argument Cocks set out in his 2004 book, *The Wolf At The Door*, which examines much of Kubrick's work—and life— from this perspective. Nathan Abrams [2014] further explores these themes). *Room 237* also covers the 'impossible' layout of the Overlook as a labyrinth, with Jack as its mythical Minotaur, subliminal psychosexual messages hidden throughout the film, and even the suggestion that *The Shining* is Kubrick's confession and apology for his involvement with faking footage of the 1969 moon landing.

These readings—which comb through narrative, script and visual details as if unearthing vital clues—are inevitably skewed by personal interests and ideas, and the conclusions are often supported by interpretation held up as evidence. This is, of course, the subjective nature of textual analysis, and as such no single interpretation is any more 'accurate' than another, even if some (faking the moon landing) are unquestionably absurd. Diane Johnson, addressing Cocks's reading, refutes the idea that Kubrick intended any Holocaust allusions, but offers a valuable argument: 'the whole notion that certain unconscious motifs creep into Kubrick's films the way they would in to any novelist's works, without the conscious collusion of the artist, is certainly valid' (2006:

59)—interpretation is not meant to usurp intention (and indeed, intention matters), but it is no less relevant in attempting to understand any given work. At the very least, we can appreciate films like *Room 237* as a paean to interpretative studies, and *The Shining*'s various analyses as fascinating evidence of its continued significance for genre fans, Kubrick aficionados and cinephiles, and of the film's enduring status as an object of cultish devotion (Hunter 2016, Mee 2017).

OVERLOOKING CONVENTION

In focusing on these unconventional theories, there is a of risk dismissing Kubrick's stated intentions and a number of *The Shining*'s more obvious interpretations, both of which position it as a powerful horror film. Themes all too visible on the surface of *The Shining* in part lend the film its creeping tension and eventual terror. Tropes common to the genre (and sources of real life horror) are effectively handled, and warrant detailed discussion in an effort to legitimately situate the film in the contemporary horror canon. The threat of domestic violence and the terrible father, the supernatural/knowing child, possession, isolation and claustrophobia, memories and nightmares, all connect *The Shining* to horror films which came before, and in turn, films which it subsequently influenced. Exploring these themes and connections acknowledge it as a successful genre film, which—as part of Kubrick's oeuvre—is a status it often eludes. Even in studies which analyse genre, *The Shining* is often suggested to transcend it. Walter Metz, for example, argues that the film 'offers a liminal narrational system caught between the horror film and the family melodrama which offers the possibility of critique unavailable to either of the genres in their "pure state"', and suggests that the 'the film presents both a ghost story and a horror film, a tale of the uncanny and a family melodrama' (1997: 40), as if these labels are mutually exclusive. This fails to acknowledge that the ghost story and the uncanny can be collapsed as common features of various cycles, subgenres and modes of the horror genre, rather than being genres in their own right (not to mention that we might, in this context, also count familial drama as a source of horror). Robert Kolker calls it 'more a parody of the horror genre than a film seriously intent on giving its audience a fright', even while likening it to 'many recent representatives of the genre' in its 'examination of the family' (2011: 99), and suggests the film demonstrates Kubrick mocking his audience (99, 148). Paul Mayersberg claimed the film comments on 'the facile convention of horror writing and film-making' (1980: 55), an argument demonstrative of a broader critical distaste for horror.

We can understand the hesitance to consider its obvious generic status in part as a result of Kubrick's approach to horror film making, which resulted in an aesthetic unusual to a mainstream appreciation of the form at the time. It is, of course, easier to look back at a horror film which influenced so much that came after it, and retrospectively stake a claim for its significance in the genre's history, than it might have been to understand its importance so soon after its release. The film, with its artistic approach to a commercial film formula, its ambiguous narrative and Hollywood cast, occupies an uncanny space between high and low culture (Luckhurst 2013: 27). However, appreciation of *The Shining* often relies on an understanding of how Kubrick, a veritable filmmaking genius, cleverly manipulated and ultimately transcended the superficial horror film formula, poking fun at one of the lowest generic forms and its equally lowbrow audience. These readings carry implications regarding the judgement of audience tastes and a misunderstanding of horror's cultural value and social commentaries, as well as dismissal (or ignorance) of the genre's varied approaches, cycles and conventions. Furthermore, it risks undermining *The Shining*'s horrifying effectiveness for the sake of auteurist worship, and makes assumptions about Kubrick's approach to the genre, dismissing his open claims of interest in the supernatural and his stated desire to make a horror film, as well as the commercial imperatives of the film's production.

It is clear from Kubrick's notes that he was keen to reference recognisable horror tropes. In wanting 'to make the scariest movie he could' (Johnson 2006: 55) his aim was not to mock nor waive genre conventions, but rather embrace them, albeit in a way which suited his personal style and enigmatic approach to storytelling. Pre-production notes, for all of their mentions of Freud, Bettelheim and Herman Hesse, do not support the idea that Kubrick was interested in horror only on the condition that he could coldly intellectualise it. As I have discussed, the use of parody in the film is not employed to mock the genre or its audience, but rather to emphasise its grotesque and uncanny elements—enhancing, not reducing, its horror credentials. Early scripts and handwritten notes suggest additional scenes of horror that did not make it to the final cut: sleepwalking and nightmares, Danny finding a teddy bear slashed across the gut, and glowing red eyes in the dark (SK15/1/1). Gruesome, scribbled sentences across King's manuscript imagine additional gory horrors ('I'LL GOUGE OUT YOUR EYES AND SUCK THE HOLES!' [SK/15/1/2: 401]). Throughout, the emphasis is clearly on meeting expectations:

> LIST MANIFESTATIONS ASSOCIATED WITH EVIL HOUSES. LIGHTS OUT—OR ON! DOORS SLAMMING OR OPENING. DRAFTS. KNOCKING NOISES. MUSIC. (SK/15/1/2 364)
>
> IMMORTALITY. BASIS OF GHOST AND HORROR. V. IMPORTANT (SK/15/1/2 374)

What are manifestations of a haunted house.
(1)   Noises
(2)   Things changing place
(3)   Smells
(4)   Lights on and off
(5)   Mirror reflections   (SK15/1/1)

Many of these ideas do not feature in the final film, but we are left with a number of additions: Jack's nightmare and Danny's nightmarish visions, the ghostly 1920s music (as part of a very creepy soundtrack), and the mirror reflections which raise questions about the legitimacy of the hauntings (but not Jack's acceptance of them). Unintentionally, the film also features 'things changing place': a chair behind Jack's makeshift writing desk in the Colorado Lounge disappears in one shot, and on their tour of the kitchen Halloran, Wendy and Danny step into a walk-in freezer via the same door they then leave through—but as they exit, and the film cuts back to the kitchen corridor, the shot is clearly from a different direction, using a different door, so that they appear to come out in an entirely different place. No doubt these are continuity errors, but the chair disappears during Jack's first angry outburst, and the shot of Halloran, Wendy and Danny exiting the 'wrong' door is disorienting, coming just after Wendy exclaims: 'This whole place is such an enormous maze, I feel like I'll have to leave a trail of breadcrumbs every time I come in.' The effect of both is potentially unsettling for any detail-oriented viewer. Meanwhile, the changes or additions to King's story which make it into the final cut—namely Danny's encounter with the Grady girls, the gushing blood from the elevator, the woman in 237, the replacement of Jack's roque mallet attack with his axe through the door, and his chasing Danny through the dark, freezing maze—are resolutely horrifying sequences, effective at the time of their release and now iconic.

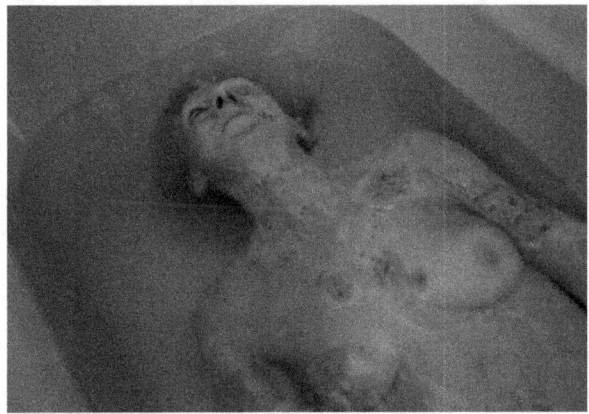

11 *The woman in 237*

The film is peppered with allusions, intentional or otherwise, to existing horror texts which suggest an appreciation of the film genre (or, at least, connect *The Shining* to it more clearly than some might wish to acknowledge). It has been linked with *Psycho* (Hitchcock, 1960), especially in its Freudian pseudo-psychological explanations, bathroom-set scenes of terror, and Wendy and Jack's battle on the stairwell (Titterington 1981, Mayersberg 1980, Jameson 1981, Metz 1997). Stephen King's inspiration in writing *The Shining* came in part from Shirley Jackson's novel *The Haunting of Hill House* (1959) (Norden 1983), and both adaptations (Jackson's book provided the basis for *The Haunting* [Wise, 1963]) can be connected through their studies of mental breakdown and psychic ability, as well as their labyrinthine haunted houses—indeed, the Overlook and its vast grounds, isolated on a mountain top, with its empty, creepy corridors and grand open spaces, resembles 'the Old Dark House of American horror films' (Titterington 1981: 120). Titterington also notices how the corpse rising from the bathtub recollects *Diabolique* (Clouzot, 1955)—with clear visual clues in the shot of the still water over a deathly face, and a hand gripping the rim of the bath, in a scene which also features a shocking discovery on a typewriter. Jack's dragging limp as he chases Danny through the maze 'recalls all those horror film cripples and hunchbacks of the nineteen thirties, just as Wendy's vision of cobwebs and skeletons [...] revives one of the genre's hoariest devices' (Nelson 1982: 203-204). The woman in 237, once she transforms from a sexual fantasy figure to a decaying crone, walks towards Jack with her arms outstretched to him, her movements as stilted as a Romero zombie or Frankenstein's monster. The bathtub corpse also features in *Repulsion* (Polanski, 1965), which, similarly to *The Shining*, ends with a shot of a photograph that provides some explanations while raising a number of other questions. Danny's shining connects him with a number of telepathic or 'seeing' children (most obviously, with the sympathetic 'Other' of *Carrie*), and by initially presenting his power as something with the potential for evil, more loosely associates the film with a number featuring demonic, possessed or plain creepy children including *Village of the Damned* (Rilla, 1960), *The Innocents* (Clayton, 1961), *Who Can Kill A Child?* (Serrador, 1976), *The Brood* (Cronenberg, 1979), *The Omen*, and *The Exorcist*. Kubrick's use of colour and pattern recalls the arty euro-horror of *Suspiria* (Argento, 1977), while the Steadicam tracking and shots from Jack's point of view in room 237 are aligned with the style of the slasher cycle popularised by *Halloween* (Carpenter, 1978). Kubrick reportedly screened *Eraserhead* (Lynch, 1977) for his cast and crew as an example of the weird, unsettling tone he wanted to emulate (Leigh 2017) and the final film's mainstream gloss and serious approach to horror is similar to some of the previous decade's most successful horror films, including *The Exorcist* and *Rosemary's Baby*.

There are some clear intertextual references in the film then, but there are also a number of more significant thematic connections on the film's surface level. Paul Mayersberg argued that 'to take *The Shining* at its face value is a mistake. It has no face, only masks, and it has no value, only implications' (1980: 253). I disagree. While there is much to be said (and much *has* been said) about the film's allusive (and elusive) nature, and there is a certain satisfaction in solving its various puzzles, the most obvious readings tell us a great deal about intention and inspiration. Its themes, both on its surface and just below, tie it to a rich history of horror, but also mark it as very much of its moment. *The Shining* can be aligned with contemporaneous horror trends which, at face value, connect it to the genre (rather than distancing it by insisting on hidden meanings), and these clear themes are as terrifying in their immediacy as anything offered to the subconscious.

KEEPING IT IN THE FAMILY

The Shining can be connected to *Psycho* through more than its bathroom and staircase scenes. Hitchcock's film has long been credited as a turning point for the genre, a moment when popular horror's monsters were more clearly configured as 'one of us' than ever before, and the first Hollywood feature which 'recognised Horror as both American and familial' (Wood 1979: 19). There are as many differences between the films, and between psychopathic mommy's boy Norman Bates (Anthony Perkins) and Jack Torrance as there are similarities, but their commitment to running their respective hostelries, their dedication to the Overlook's and Bates Motel's ghostly proprietors, the violent manifestations of their repressed sexuality, their troubled family pasts and their swiftly eroding sanity warrant the comparison. Hitchcock's refusal to explain Norman's motivation until the final sequence, via the psychiatrist (Simon Oakland) ('He was never all Norman, but he was often only Mother'), offers an entirely human, psychological rationale which Grady's unlocking of the pantry door ultimately denies *The Shining*. But the option of seeing supernatural or psychological motivations for Norman and Jack's behaviour is similar throughout the rest of both narratives, and neither conclusion detracts from the horrors of which violent men are capable. Norman and Jack are both terrifyingly human, however we choose to understand their possession. For Wendy and Danny, the horrors of the Overlook are glimpsed in its various ghostly manifestations, but it is Jack's slipping mask of sanity, his potential wrath, and the tensions between the Torrances which provokes true terror. Diane Johnson acknowledged that themes of 'family hate' were central to the adaptation, and Jack Nicholson, in promotion for the film, also connected it to the era's broader cultural concerns: 'If you take a sociological view of the last ten years, you'd find that the most volatile element in our culture is the pressure inside the family unit' (in Baxter 1997: 34). As Kubrick himself described, above all else *The Shining* is 'the story of one man's family quietly going insane together' (in Hofsess 1980).

Critiques of the American family were prevalent in much horror of the late 1960s and 1970s. What *Psycho*—and, in the UK, *Peeping Tom*—had pre-empted with their studies of the troubling results of traumatic, past parent-child relationships evolved in to more immediate reflections of the disintegrating institution of the nuclear family. Birth rates dropped significantly in the late 1960s following the post-War baby boom, new federal legislations saw a rise in divorce and separation, and more people opted to live single or childless lives (Cook 2002: 294). While the nuclear family remained very much the conservative ideological norm in the US, it is unsurprising that horror cinema began to reflect on these changes in lifestyle just as other genres of the New Hollywood period had. Many horror films began to openly criticise the traditional family unit or show its collapse. *Rosemary's Baby* depicts a paranoid young woman in a deceitful marriage, and the horror of pregnancy, childbirth and motherhood. *Night of the Living Dead* (Romero, 1968) sees families destroyed, and a young girl devour her parents. *Carrie*'s true horror stems from the taut relationship between Carrie White (Sissy Spacek) and a controlling, pious mother (Piper Laurie) who would rather see her daughter dead than shamed, and the film concludes with matricide and the 'literal collapse of the family home' (Mitchell 2013: 49). *The Exorcist*'s 12-year-old Regan MacNeil (Linda Blair) is possessed in the midst of her mother's acrimonious divorce from a father conspicuously absent. The psychic, deformed children of *The Brood* are mothered by a woman (abused by her own parents as child) embroiled in a custody battle for her human child. *The Hills Have Eyes* (Craven, 1977) pits an all-American nuclear family against a troop of related mutants, ironically flipping their 'good' and 'bad' statuses. The parody of the American family in *The Texas Chain Saw Massacre* relies on a horrible black comedy similar to Kubrick's strategy of grotesque humour; Jack's 'Wendy, I'm home' and 'Here's Johnny' are reminiscent in tone to *Chain Saw*'s patriarch (Jim Siedow), arriving home with his (presumed) son (Edwin Neal) and a screaming, struggling, Sally (Marilyn Burns) to find the entrance carved up by Leatherface's (Gunnar Hansen) chainsaw, exclaiming with perfect comic delivery, 'Look what your brother did to the door!'.

The Shining's strongest comparisons with this wave of familial terror can be found in *The Amityville Horror* (Rosenberg, 1979), also an adaptation of a popular 1977 novel (by Jay Anson), based on the real-life case of a family who move into a new home, only to flee after a month, citing hauntings by the previous inhabitants who were murdered by their eldest son (the murders were real, the hauntings disputed). The film's patriarch George Lutz (James Brolin) becomes possessed by the house's spirits, including the ghosts of Shinnecock Native Americans who occupy the burial ground in the house's foundations. He insists his family need to be 'disciplined', much like Jack's must be 'corrected'. The Lutz's young daughter shares a connection with the home's ghosts, notably its dead children—unlike Danny Torrance, she does not resist the temptation to 'come and play', and makes friends with one particularly malevolent entity. Kathy (Margot Kidder) has nightmares of George murdering her and her daughter with his axe, a dream that almost comes true on the Lutz's last night in the house. There are numerous examples of horror's 'coming home' then, and of the ways in which the genre tackled familial, marital and generational conflicts through the decade preceding *The Shining*'s production and release, which provide apt comparison. And yet, the film was subject to tenuous connections with divorce melodrama *Kramer vs. Kramer* (Benton, 1979), (Mayersberg 1980, Kroll 1980, Keeler 1981) in place of linking it to the trends of the genre, and at the risk of removing the centrality of its domestic violence theme as its most obvious surface horror.

Patriarchal violence or abuse—or otherwise ineffectual, absent or neglectful husbands and fathers—is a common theme in King's work and its various adaptations (e.g. *It, Dolores Claiborne, Rose Madder, Needful Things*) (see Magistrale 2003), and a number of Kubrick's films addressed issues of gender, male roles and responsibilities and the deviant or violent behaviour stemming from these (e.g. *Full Metal Jacket, Lolita, A Clockwork Orange, Eyes Wide Shut*). *The Shining* is arguably the clearest example of these themes across both authors' works. Jack's abusive tendencies are more apparent in the original cut of the film released in North America, in the scene where Wendy discusses his drunken assault on Danny with the doctor, explaining his actions ('he wasn't in the greatest mood that night'), justifying them and defending her husband ('it was just one of those things, y'know, purely an accident'). Her shaking hand as she lights her cigarette, twitching smile and over-cheerful tone betray her fear, and the doctor's reaction—silent, her flat expression making it clear that she does not concur the injury was 'just one of those things'—emphasises Wendy's discomfort. We see a similar response later on in both cuts, this time to her husband, when Jack turns on her after she interrupts his writing:

> Wendy, let me explain something to you: when you come in here and interrupt me you're breaking my concentration, you're distracting me [he slaps his forehead], and it will then take me time to get back to where I was [he rips a typed page in two]. Understand? [...] Fine. We're gonna make a new rule. Whenever I'm in here, and you hear me typing [he grins, condescendingly, and hammers the typewriter keys], or

whether you don't hear me typing, or whatever the fuck you hear me doing in here, when I'm in here, that means I'm working. That means don't come in. Now, do you think you can handle that? [...] Fine. Then why don't you start right now and get the fuck out of here?[8]

Jack's sudden changes in behaviour (both here and following the incident in 237, where he goes from reassuring to accusatory in a second), rather than a confusingly unmotivated character flaw, are the potentially violent mood swings of an abuser—a status he himself later confesses, complete with horrible actions, to Lloyd. Pausing, placating him, speaking in soft tones so as not to anger him further, Wendy appears shocked by his snapping, but her expression is tinged with a sad familiarity, and she accepts his anger quietly and calmly, just as she has before, 'because like so many other women in her position, she really has no choice' (Cook 1984: 4). While we are only privy to Jack's physical attacks on Danny, it would not be a stretch to imagine similar assaults on his wife of the nature he later promises with his threat to 'bash [her] brains in'. Jack's cruel emotional and verbal abuse, and his lack of respect or care for Wendy is obvious, and her fear of her husband is apparent throughout.

12 Preparing for the worst

Much has been made of Duvall's casting as Wendy and the well-documented tension on set with a frustrated Kubrick who pushed beyond her limits (most famously seen in Vivian Kubrick's behind-the-scenes documentary footage). Diane Johnson has lamented the strained relationship, and felt that, in Kubrick cutting a number of Duvall's lines, 'the result was not the "round" Wendy as I had hoped to characterize her (and so did King), but a moist character reduced to tears and whimpers' (2006: 57-58). Kubrick, who rather unfairly noted that, in comparison to the novel's Wendy, Duvall seemed 'exactly the kind of woman that would marry Jack and be stuck with him' (in Ciment 1980: 484), had also suggested to Nicholson early in the production that Wendy's part required someone 'that maybe the audience would also like to kill a little bit' (in Pierce 2009: 191). In analyses, Duvall's casting is often explained via misogynistic value judgements of the actor's appearance and mannerisms: Duvall is 'not a sexually attractive woman and therefore plays the film's role as Danny's protective mother better than she could the novel's as Jack's lover' (Nelson 1982: 216); her Wendy is 'neither attractive nor bright [...] her quirky mannerisms and nondescript appearance superbly capture the sense of despair and disappointment that makes Wendy's existence so depressing' (Manchel 1995: 74). The casting choice, if intended to provoke viewers' annoyance, seems effective then, but at a cost: Jack's threat to 'bash [her] brains in' 'taps in to a vague irritation the audience has been encouraged to feel about Wendy, almost pushing the film into overt misogyny' (Naremore 2007: 201). The final character might not be as fully fleshed out as Johnson hoped, and may well trigger irritation for certain viewers, but if anything, this surely compounds the unsettling premise of being encouraged to identify with Jack. Duvall's performance strengthens a character who risks being seen as merely meek. She is not the 'screaming dishrag' Stephen King saw, but a terrified, confused and exhausted woman protecting her son—a long-suffering abused wife, married to a man with a history of violence, with experience of placating and pleasing him for her family's safety. Duvall appropriately plays along, Wendy feebly keeping the peace and excusing Jack until it becomes clear he might well have hurt Danny again (at which point, without further discussion, she immediately moves both herself and Danny away from 'son of a bitch' Jack). Sharon Marie Carnicke (2006) outlines a fascinating comparison of Duvall's and Nicholson's physical performances, which offer extremes at either end of the spectrum positioning them as villain (or monster) and victim—Nicholson's movements 'big', his expressions elaborate, his movements extreme and exaggerated, while Duvall uses minimal space on screen, making Wendy's reactions authentic and nuanced. As Jack becomes more violent, losing his mind as the Overlook takes it over, so Wendy becomes more exhausted, more desperate, more emotional (while simultaneously becoming more resourceful and protective, as the situation demands). Duvall's portrayal of Wendy's terror is, by the film's final scenes, horrifyingly realistic, her screams prompting an audience's visceral reaction as Jack hacks at the bathroom door and we, like Wendy, can only watch, cower and wait.

13 'Wendy, I'm home'

Wendy's earlier strategy of 'playing along' with Jack is also apparent in the relationship between him and Danny. Their conversations are cold and their interactions distanced. Wendy and Danny are frequently seen together—talking, playing, watching television, happy in each other's company. Aside from Danny leading Jack in to the maze, he and his father are only alone together for one scene, a tense, foreboding exchange in which they both lie about their feelings. Going to the caretaker's apartment to fetch a toy fire engine, Danny is warned by his mother not to disturb a sleeping Jack. Creeping in carefully, he finds his father awake, dishevelled, sitting on the bed and staring blankly in to the distance. Jack reaches out for him, lifts him on to his lap and into an awkward, stiff embrace. They have a cautious conversation, slow and staged, Jack playing the role of the concerned father but with the vacant stare and creeping grin of a man possessed. Danny asks his father if he likes the Overlook and Jack replies that 'I love it... I want you to like it here, I wish we could stay here forever and ever and ever'. The line ties Jack's wish to that of the Grady girls in wanting Danny dead so they can play with him at the Overlook 'forever and ever', and in turn provides a sinister double meaning to the 'play' that Jack expresses a desire for in his repeated written complaint that 'all work and no play make Jack a dull boy'. The exact nature of Jack's 'work' and his 'play' are sinisterly vague and open to interpretation, 'since the most important work of the Overlook's caretaker is the play of murdering his family' (Magistrale 2003: 97). Jack tells Danny that he cannot sleep, he has 'too much to do'. 'You would never hurt mommy and me, would you?' Danny asks. 'I love you, Danny. I love you more than anything else in the whole world. I would never do anything to hurt you,' Jack promises. Danny, of course, does not need to rely on his shining to make the connection between the dead girls and his strangely acting father, nor to think about the hand gripping his arm to know that it is untrue that his dad would never hurt him; he already broke that arm. Jack's later confession to Lloyd, using the same language—he loves Danny, would never hurt him—confirms the incident and pre-empts its recurrence. But the boy realises that, in order to avoid being consigned to play at the Overlook forever, he must at least play along with his father's fantasy for now.

14 'I would never do anything to hurt you'

Jack's anger and violence, and the resulting interactions with his wife and child, while correlating with the Overlook's haunting, can be understood within the context of contemporaneous horror as a reflection on the generational, familial and gender tensions at play at the time. The film was in production at the end of the 1970s and released in a US election year which saw a landslide victory for Ronald Reagan and a figurative return to Republican conservatism—straddling two ostensibly distinct, but ultimately unclear and tumultuous periods in American social history. Sexual revolution and feminist progress had empowered young people and especially young women, highlighting alternatives to traditional pathways of marriage, homemaking and childrearing, but simultaneously 'dislocated male identities dependent on other fixed points of reference for their map of self-meaning' (Kellner and Ryan 1988: 172). Jack is still clearly the Torrance's breadwinner, and Wendy the family homemaker responsible for cooking, cleaning and childcare—but Jack's employment at the Overlook (at least as far as his contract with Ullman goes) is semantic. His status as caretaker commands remuneration and a roof over the family's head, but it is Wendy who 'takes care' of the family and, most notably, Jack's official work. Wendy is seen keeping records of checks on the boiler (a nod to King's narrative trope) and keeping in touch with the police down the mountain. Jack may rant about his obligations to the Overlook ('Have you ever thought for a single solitary moment about my responsibilities to my employers… the owners have placed their complete confidence and trust in me…I have signed a contract…has it ever occurred to you what would happen to my future if I failed to live up to my responsibilities?'), but he has made himself redundant by ignoring them. Meanwhile, the writing he initially sees as his real work is rendered pointless by the meaningless repetition of an unoriginal line handed to him by the hotel's spirits. Jack is emotionally stunted, creatively blocked, and, we presume, physically and sexually frustrated as a result of the repression of his desires.

So Jack's truest purpose becomes murder, busy work intertwined with and indistinguishable from the appealing play the hotel's spirits offer him, the 'business we discussed', as Grady reminds him. His conservative patriarchal need to manage or 'correct' his family is combined with his obligations to the Overlook, and both offer the satisfaction of an enjoyable job well done. Reasserting his patriarchal authority and reinstating (by force) his role offers a number of enticing results—revenge for being relegated to financier rather than leader of the Torrance family, the pleasure of giving in to baser instincts, and the promise of praise from his true, supernatural employers, or even the opportunity for promotion (what 'caretaker' appears in a tuxedo at the centre of a well-heeled party crowd in a commemorative photo deemed special enough to be framed and hung for future guests to see?). In allowing Jack a multi-faceted role which combines labour and responsibility with authority and status, the Overlook becomes more than his employer:

> Symbolically, The Overlook becomes Jack's other Home and other Family, a nightmare world of dismemberment and alienation (where 'sliced peaches' and 'Heinz Ketchup' recall family massacres, not family meals), in which the mother and child are victims of the father's desire to cannibalize one family to ensure the 'survival' of another, to violate one home to resuscitate the corpse of another. (Nelson 1982: 307-308)

The hotel is not just *another* home and family, though. For Jack, it is a preferable alternative, which offers him purpose, respect and superficial rewards in its promise of sex and booze in lavish surroundings—just out of reach until he destroys his present family life and stays 'forever and ever'. The woman in 237 remains a corpse and the Jack Daniels bottle stays under Lloyd's control until Jack's work is complete. It is telling that his final assault on his family takes place in the caretaker's apartment where they are based during their stay. Compared to the grandeur of the Gold Room or the vast openness and plushness of the Colorado Lounge, where much of Jack's new work and play occurs, the apartment is small, drab, and restrictive, a home from home—limiting for Jack, comfortable for Wendy. During the Torrances' orientation on closing day, Jack can barely conceal his dismay, glancing over its twee, floral-papered walls and observing, 'perfect for a child… cosy… it's very, uh, homey'. Conversely, Wendy, although sharing Jack's initial polite disappointment, seems entirely more at home in the apartment as the family settle than she does in the public spaces, which are intimidatingly grand and empty. We have seen her and Danny comfortable in their similarly-sized apartment in Boulder, and Wendy is at ease in the Overlook's equivalent. She retreats to its safety in later scenes while Jack roams the hotel. During the baseball bat scene he demands, 'What are you doing down here?!' clearly demarcating their private spaces. 'I just want to go back to my room', she sobs as the fight intensifies. The apartment, little more to Jack than servants' quarters, is attached to a 'real life' from which he cannot quite escape, and it represents his stifled role in his corporeal family. Breaking down the front door and exclaiming 'Wendy, I'm home!' offers more than sitcom parody (Smith 1997:

303)—it is an attempt to figuratively violate the Torrance household, and a sign of Jack's commitment to his new Overlook family in their grand mountainside mansion. However, his failure to destroy and replace his real family supports Vivian Sobchack's assertion that, in the era's horror cinema:

> there seems no viable way for patriarchy to symbolically envision a satisfying future for itself. All it can do is deny the future. There is no narrative resolution for patriarchy in the horror film—except the denial or death of the father, finally impotent and subject to the present power of his own horrific past. (1996: 159)

We cannot be certain if Jack's anticlimactic, impotent demise in the freezing maze marks the end of his time at the Overlook, but we know, as both Grady and the photograph tell us, that in some way or another he has 'always been' there. That the photograph is of Jack, surrounded by partygoers, rather than the picture of the Torrance family sat around a table at the hotel, which Jack finds in early scripts, speaks to his desire to get away from his Torrance family and make a new Overlook one (SK/15/1/19: 5). Wanting to regress and unable to realise a happy future because of his nostalgic desire for a lifestyle belonging to a bygone era, Jack is trapped and ultimately defeated by his own horrific present family life.

SCRATCHING THE SURFACE

Jack's 'looking back' is configured through more than his attitude to home and family, and forms part of a complex approach to history in *The Shining*, which finds much of the film's horror in the transgressions of the past and the threat of repetition, as well as themes of racism and class division. The Overlook influences Jack in his regression from the polite, amenable, educated (and presumably—as a 1970s college professor—liberal) man seen in his interview with Ullman, to the caveman who hobbles in to the hedge maze after Danny, only to become trapped and die like an animal. Along the way, Jack's mask of civility gradually slips. Meeting Ullman on closing day, he reads a copy of *Playgirl* openly in the lobby, and chats to the new employer he has met once through a mouthful of food. As he distances himself further from Wendy and Danny, he connects obnoxiously with Lloyd and Grady, their exchanges shrouded in the crass humour and outdated attitudes of an old barroom drunk before Jack even takes a sip of bourbon (his Faustian offering of his soul for 'just a glass of beer' recalling a regular's plea for 'just one more drink' after being told he has had enough). He is misogynistic, referring to Wendy as 'that bitch' and 'the old sperm bank upstairs'. 'Women. Can't live with 'em, can't live without 'em,' Lloyd retorts, in the flat tone of someone used to telling his customers exactly what they want to hear.[9] Jack's sexist, racist hatred is stirred up by white men, and his resulting violence targets women, children (George Hatfield is left out of the film's narrative, but the boy was seventeen), and notably, in the film's only murder, an African-American.

In the red bathroom, Grady and Jack's conversation connects Wendy and Danny as a disobedient family unit who need to be 'corrected' ('Perhaps they need a good talking to, if you don't mind my saying so, perhaps a bit more'), planting the seed for Jack's attempted killing spree. This talk has progressed from an already sinister path as Grady informs Jack that Danny is telepathically communicating with Dick Halloran, attempting to bring him back to the hotel to help. The conversation sets Halloran further apart as an exception who, as an 'outside party' (an 'Other') represents a specific threat to the Torrance-Overlook family's particular 'situation'. This outside party, Grady explains with visible and audible disgust, is a 'nigger [...] a nigger cook', the connection and the racist label configuring Halloran as inferior in all aspects: race, class, and his role as both a labouring 'cook' (not, we note, a 'chef', as would be suitable for a hotel of the Overlook's calibre, and as Ullman refers to him earlier) and an 'outsider'. Jack pauses on hearing the word for the first time, appearing uncomfortable, even disbelieving. He lowers his head slowly and raises his eyebrows, taking a moment before trying it out for himself, repeating it (too) comfortably: Grady, with his 'proper' British accent and his haughtiness, has given Jack permission to allow his suppressed racism (already hinted at with his earlier 'white man's burden' aside to Lloyd) to rise to the surface (Naremore 2007: 201; Metz 1997: 54; Smith 1997: 302; Jameson 1980: 32). Misogyny and racism is not just *welcomed* in the swinging Gold Room parties; Jack's patriarchal, white supremacist rage is actively *encouraged*, essential for acceptance into the Overlook's family. Murdering Wendy, Danny and Halloran is a horrible test which will initiate Jack in to the hotel's spiritual club.

The stereotype which Halloran fulfils is an issue with *The Shining*'s characterisation, which would exist even if not highlighted by Jack's simmering racism (and Grady's overt prejudice). The role of a 'helper' who exists to guide or support protagonists is a common narratological figure, and so in this context, an essential aide to Danny (see previous chapter). However, when this helper is a black character who is dispensable beyond the assistance they offer a white character (especially through magic or mysticism—like Dick's shining), the figure becomes a stereotype. There are obvious derogatory implications in Kubrick's framing Dick Halloran as a 'simple, rustic type' whose 'folksy character and naïve attempts to explain telepathy to Danny makes what he has to say dramatically more acceptable than a standard pseudo-scientific explanation. He and Danny make a good pair' (quoted in Webster 2011: 111). Understood this way, Halloran is less a helper to Danny, and more aligned with him as 'simple', 'folksy', 'naïve'—a racist reduction of a black man as childish (further unfair given Dick's presumed witnessing of the historical horrors of the Overlook), which makes his death all the more troubling. Halloran's 'purpose' is more fulfilled in King's book where he survives the Overlook and completes his rescue mission; the character is one of a number of 'magical negroes' in the author's work (see Okorafor 2004 for discussion). Kubrick's Halloran is judged for being expendable (more accurately, Kubrick is judged for making him expendable): critic Pauline Kael suggested that 'the awful suspicion pops into the mind that since we don't want Wendy or Danny hurt, and there's no-one else alive around for Jack to get at, he's given the black man' (quoted in Naremore 2007: 201), and Dennis Bingham argues that 'Kubrick's confused attitude toward women is compounded with his confused attitude toward blacks: he seems not to have thought very much about either' (1996: 305). It is true that Halloran 'got it', as Diane Johnson indelicately phrased, because she and Kubrick felt a grisly death needed to be included in their horror film. Narratively speaking, it makes sense that the victim is Halloran, who knows something is wrong (rather than, for example, Ullman, whose return would be unmotivated). But his death, coupled with the stereotyping (compounded by the potentially monstrous vision of him as a 'figure of savagery' when possessed in early scripts; see previous chapter), provide support for these interpretations of racism.

There are significant issues with representation in *The Shining* then, but the film is 'decidedly unconfused in its attitude to America's racism' (Webster 2011: 111), and we should consider that Halloran's death can be interpreted as emphasising these undercurrents. The readings of allusions to large-scale historical atrocities such as the Holocaust and Native American genocide are tied by threads of racism and perceived racial superiority, and Jack's axe-murder of Halloran offers a figurative realisation of systemic white violence. Furthermore, taken at face value, Jack and his instructors are clearly evil, and Halloran our sympathetic-cum-tragic hero. Walter Metz likens Halloran's death with the 'absurd' murder of Ben (Duane Jones) in *Night of the Living Dead* as a black hero who 'plays by the rules of white society and loses by forfeiting his life' (1997: 57-58). There is a connection, but the suggestion that Halloran is 'punished' on account of his race (something Metz claims, using *Living Dead* as an example, is typical to horror) lacks nuance. Ben is (unlike Halloran) a protagonist with whom viewers are asked to identify, but both perform a heroic function,[10] and face a horrifying, unjust death rather than getting their own happy ending. In both films, rather than the black hero being simply dispensable, their death renders the realist, senseless horror of racism potentially more frightening than any zombie horde or axe murderer. Halloran's death (rather than his possession proposed in the original script), underlines Jack's disturbing regression. In turn, this emphasis on overt racism furthers the uncanny and uncomfortable nature of *The Shining*'s horror. Inclination depending, viewers can ignore the racism of Halloran's murder, or be forced to question its meaning; either result is appalling in its implication.

In addition to the film's horror being found in racial inequality, it also exists in the representation of class divisions. Kellner and Ryan argue that 'Kubrick uses the occult story as an instrument for analysing the sort of breakdown that occurs when interpersonal structures like the family are forced to absorb the negative feelings of aggression and resentment generated by an economic system that unequally distributes success, gratification, and a sense of self-worth' (1988:173), and furthermore, that family life in the late 1970s had become a less appealing option than 'a post-industrial culture of increased leisure and an expanding singles life' (172). In other words, Jack, who lost his teaching job and is clearly struggling as a writer, resents his family on account of their holding him back—and the Overlook, with all of the opulence and opportunity associated with aristocratic comfort, represents what they are holding him back from. Jack does not view himself as a working-class labourer; he outwardly rejects and resents the idea of 'shovelling out driveways, working in a carwash' instead of working at the hotel; when Wendy suggests they leave for Danny's sake, he rants 'I have let you fuck up my life this far, but I am not going to let you fuck this up'. Of course, he has taken a role as a caretaker, but it is a cover for his writing, and he only becomes interested in his 'obligations' to his employer once the perks of the job are clear.

The Overlook's ghosts do not choose Jack to do their dirty work for much reason other than the fact that he is susceptible to their suggestions. His alcoholism, violent history and suppressed, bubbling resentment toward his family make him more impressionable even than Danny, whose shining abilities no doubt make him an attractive prospect for the hotel's spirits, but who has enough good sense and childish fear to reject them. The Overlook knows how to appeal to Jack's baser vices, promising him sex and alcohol as perks of the more indulgent upper-class lifestyle of which he feels deserving. When Jack is in control of his supernatural fantasies, his position as valued guest or caretaker-manager is clear (the meaning of 'caretaker' fluctuates, from the residential janitor position that brings the Torrances to the Overlook, to a loftier overseer at the heart of the 4th July festivities, via Grady as butler/instructor). There is no judgement of his indiscretions past (drinking, breaking Danny's arm) or present (infidelity, racism, bad jokes), and Lloyd and Grady condone his arrogance, and mollify and feed his ego ('No charge to you, Mr. Torrance'; 'You're the important one, sir'). Jack's interactions with the spirits begin warmly; the beautiful woman in 237 approaches and embraces him without question, Lloyd greets him as a regular, Grady apologises profusely for spilling advocaat on the jacket Jack intended to change 'before the fish and goose soiree'. There is enough promise here of the decadence and respect Jack craves—but things switch as soon as he becomes too comfortable. The woman in 237 has tricked him and turns in to a rotting old corpse mid-kiss (to add insult to injury, she laughs at him). Lloyd instructs him to 'drink up, Mr Torrance' and informs him that whoever pays for his drinks is 'not a matter for your concern'. Grady flips (a trait which further connects the two men, as we have already seen Jack's behaviour swing) from a fawning servant tolerating Jack's insistence that he killed his family ('That's strange sir, I don't have any recollection of that at all') to stern reminders that Jack has 'always been the caretaker', and later, dismay that he has failed to take care of 'the business we discussed'. Jack, for all the status he desires, remains a caretaker-janitor, and is put back in his place by Grady for his final task, a gruelling, physically demanding 'taking care of business'. That Jack himself does not survive the job plays a significant part in the suggestion that the film 'develops a class critique by exposing the American Dream as a cruel myth' (Metz 1997: 52)—the suggestion that one can, with hard work and a resolute spirit, find success and achieve the happy, comfortable lifestyle they long for is never realised, for Wendy and Danny in addition to Jack.

15 Two caretakers

In the opulence of the Overlook Hotel, and its well-dressed 1920s party-going ghosts, *The Shining* shares gothic tendencies toward a 'latent, romanticised nostalgia for a lost aristocratic world', even as it eschews its expected visual style—avoiding dark castles and shadowy corners and replacing them with the trappings of a true age of excess, 'the building's luxury feed[ing] Jack's resentment of his family and his fantasies of becoming a playboy author in the mould of Scott Fitzgerald' (Naremore 2007: 193). The significance of the period Jack returns to in his supernatural fantasies is clear. It offers the opportunity to join an:

> American leisure class [who] led an aggressive and ostentatious public existence [...] [and] projected a class-conscious and unapologetic image of itself without guilt, openly and armed with its emblems of top-hat and champagne glass, on the social stage in full view of the other classes [...] This is clearly a 'return of the repressed' with a vengeance: a Utopian impulse which scarcely lends itself to the usual complacent

and edifying celebration, which finds its expression in the very snobbery and class consciousness we naively suppose it to threaten. (Jameson 1981: 123).

The appeal is simple. Rather than stick with his current ill-defined and frustrating middle-class-on-the-slide status, Jack can return to a time when men deserving of stature (as he no doubt sees himself) could revel in style, unjudged and welcome to say and do as they please, free from the limitations of family life and working-to-live. The Overlook might offer Jack a new (if rather old fashioned) home, but it is a home quite different from his corporeal family one, offering less (eventual) responsibility, and eternal good times.

The tensions between past, present and future are deeply intertwined in *The Shining*, and all offer nuanced sources of fear for the individual members of the Torrance family. The past looks beautiful to Jack, furthering its appeal; the Gold Room and surrounding areas are lavishly decorated in rich golds and deep reds, the tuxedoes well pressed and the dresses adorned with fringe and sequins, the men well-groomed and the women made up and polished. The present, meanwhile, is associated with gaudy patterned carpets, drab floral wallpaper in the caretaker's apartment, and Wendy's unkempt style. Conversely, the past manifests itself horribly for Wendy and Danny (the Grady girls, the skeletons, the bloodied man and the messy aftermath of the party, the dogman and Harry), as it represents the threat of Jack returning to his past drunkenness and violent outbursts. Wendy is optimistic about the future and the family's opportunity to bond at the hotel, but for Danny, who shines forward as well as back, the future too often means a horrible premonition; 'REDRUM' is a cautionary note as well as a reference to the hotel's history, a message from the past presented backwards, which only makes sense when viewed in the mirror. There is an uncanny familiarity with the ghosts throughout— the girls know Danny's name, and Jack and Lloyd are clearly acquainted, suggesting he might represent his past, alcoholic self. Grady reminds Jack that the both of them have 'always been here', and even though Jack cannot remember this, and Grady cannot initially remember 'correcting' his family, he seems to accept that he is doomed to repeat the fate of this strange double who embodies his future. 'He must forget his past failures and inadequacies as a father, husband, and man of enlightenment; he must forget those responsibilities that bind him to Wendy and Danny; he must forget himself as Jack Torrance in present time' (Nelson 1982: 222). The possibility of staying at the Overlook 'forever and ever' (Jack in the photograph, Grady's eternal presence, the Grady girls) was significant to the supernatural tale Kubrick wanted to tell, and references to the inclusion of immortality, as the basis of horror, feature in his notes (SK/15/1/2: 374) The cyclical nature of past events repeating themselves is ever present in *The Shining*, but this is of course the very nature of hauntings; at the heart of the ghost story (and horror more broadly) is the threat and the fear of things long dead, repetition, returned repression and the nightmares of the past.

***

The Shining, in its themes of family trauma and domestic violence, racial and class tension, all connected through the film's approach to the horror of history, has been criticised for seemingly reducing the supernatural focus of King's book and replacing it with a more human evil. Like these varied themes and any one of the potential alternative readings, however, the emphasis is ultimately left to the viewer's subjective interpretation. The result, as ever, is the uncertain tone which emphasises the film's horror:

> [...] nothing here is black and white except for the racist and sexist ideology of the Overlook's vulgar fantasy world. Kubrick, it seems, knows that this is indeed the case, and by ultimately throwing this ambiguity back onto the audience, by making it our responsibility to find our way out of the maze, he has created a film in *The Shining* that is not only a remarkable achievement, but a profoundly disturbing cultural mirror. (Smith 1997: 305)

As a white, male, middle-class monster, Jack is clearly not representative of the 'return of the repressed' of Wood's 'golden age' of American horror—but neither is the film akin to the horror of a more conservative era. Produced at the end of one social period and released at the start of another, its themes examine a kickback to liberal social attitudes, problematising rather than excusing Jack's reactionary nature and denying him sympathy. *The Shining* might not quite 'fit' with the independent, low-budget cycle of 1970s American horror cinema which saw the emergence of a new wave of genre auteurs, but it can nonetheless be aligned with a number of that cycle's social allusions, and it be would be remiss to remove the film from this context. Ultimately, Kubrick made *The Shining* with the intention of achieving commercial success, and looked to the horror genre to achieve this. *The Shining*'s generic conventions and credentials cannot (and should not) be ignored.

FOOTNOTES

8. Jack Nicholson has stated that this scene was in part inspired by an exchange between him and his wife at the time, Sandra Knight, which contributed to the couple's divorce (in Pierce 2009: 192).
9. Of the scene, Turkel said: 'I wanted to be pleasantly sarcastic. That was in my mind. I was also thinking that this Jack guy is a prick and he's outta his fuckin' mind, but he's a patron and I have to humor him' (Turkel in Bozung 2015: 379).
10. Although Halloran does not physically stop Jack, and is killed before finding Danny and Wendy, his arrival in the noisy Snowcat distracts Jack as he is hacking his way in to the bathroom, and diffuses the situation, allowing Wendy to escape.

Chapter 4: Release, Reception and Cultural Legacy

When *The Shining* was released, it did not immediately receive the acclaim that many expected, and which it has since garnered. Eagerly anticipated as Kubrick's failsafe return to form following *Barry Lyndon*, it was instead met with lukewarm reviews, disappointing many fans of the filmmaker's earlier work. Critic Mark Jacobson (2013) has described how, among he and his fellow cineastes on their first viewing, 'the verdict was that the great Stanley, egghead avatar of Cold War cool, had gone terminally corny midway through *A Clockwork Orange*, halfway through the 'Singin' in the Rain' scene. *The Shining* seemed the final nail in the suddenly square-shape coffin'. Many reviewers were perplexed by Nicholson's and Duvall's performances (seen as respectively excessive or insipid), and lamented Kubrick's apparent inability to navigate the standards of the horror genre, as well as his mishandling of the chilling source material. As with much of Kubrick's work, however, the film has been critically reappraised over the decades since its release. *The Shining* is now celebrated, not only as one of the greatest horror movies ever made, but a contemporary classic in its own right. Its place in pop culture has been enshrined by endless *homage* and parody, and the film's influence on contemporary horror is ubiquitous. Revisiting *The Shining*'s release and promotion strategies, and examining the reception, reappraisal and ultimate canonisation of the film, illustrate a number of critical reservations about the horror genre and the film's place within it—even as it continues to inspire genre audiences and filmmakers almost forty years later.

Selling *The Shining*

Kubrick's involvement at all stages of production extended to promotion, and he worked with Warner Bros. on a strategic marketing campaign designed to maximise the film's appeal to a young, mainstream audience. The original theatrical trailer featured a simple, suitably enigmatic long take of the Overlook's elevators gushing blood in slow motion until it splashed claret against the camera, gradually filling the screen. A 30 second TV spot revealed more, promising plenty of terror in a succession of haunting, wordless shots (Danny running in the moonlit maze, Jack snarling and silhouetted with his axe, Wendy nervously climbing the stairs, knife raised, Halloran's petrified stare, and a lobby full of skeletons), selected and edited by Kubrick and set to the film's score. A voice-over labelled it a 'masterpiece of modern horror' and drew attention to Nicholson and Duvall's star appeal. The advert was carefully targeted to reach the maximum number of 18-34 year olds—a crucial cinemagoing demographic—over a four week period, by repeatedly broadcasting it during popular shows such as *Saturday Night Live* (ABC, 1975-), and its potential was huge:

> It is estimated by those who devised the marketing campaign that by the fourth week of the film's release, 93 percent of all adults in the 18-to-34 age group will have seen the trailer (which Kubrick personally edited and scored) at least seven times, and that 88 percent of all households in America will have been exposed to the advertisements 10.8 times. The purpose of the campaign is two-fold: to overcome any negative criticism the film has received, and most importantly, to build a huge national audience for the movie, guaranteeing an early return on its $12 million investment. (Hofsess 1980)

The 'masterpiece of modern horror' tagline was carried over to the American poster, a striking yellow and black graphic design by Saul Bass which 'obliquely suggested auteur, genre, and, as it turned out, the modernism (or post-modernism) of the former's approach to the latter' (Bingham 1996: 290). Kubrick's control persisted during poster designs, pushing Bass 'very, very hard' through some 300 drawings, 'a hell of an experience' which 'drove [him] nuts' (Bass in LoBrutto 1997: 450). Kubrick asserted, in letters to Bass which responded to his abstract designs of mazes and eyes: 'some of these are still more "surreal" than "terror"' and 'I would like to suggest it is a film of terror—a must (and the supernatural—if possible)' (SK/15/5/2/5). Rejected gory designs by Bob Gusti (blood drops, skulls, bloody eyeballs) further underline Kubrick's emphasis on the supernatural, rather than corporeal horror, and the filmmaker's insistence that his film be marketed accordingly. The adverts, trailer and poster—which showed the film rated as R before it was even certificated, under a special arrangement between the MPAA and Kubrick (LoBrutto 1997: 450)—suggest *The Shining*'s promotion and release was orchestrated to both reach the largest possible audience while being clear about the exact kind of film it was—an enigmatic, artistic horror movie, and importantly, a Stanley Kubrick film. The campaign was, at least, anecdotally effective; the UK television trailer was moved to the post-9pm watershed following complaints to the Independent Broadcasting Authority about its 'particularly disturbing' nature (*Evening Standard*, 9/10/80, SK/15/11/1), and a concerned moviegoer sent an angry letter to the head of Warner Bros. after encountering the 'very effective' trailer before a screening of the studio's 'delightful' *Going In Style* (Brest, 1979):

> It's one of the 'scariest' trailers I've ever seen. But it is simply out of place at *Going in Style*. It ruined, for me, several of the opening scenes as I struggled to overcome the impact of the flood of blood. But I wonder if you really care. I suspect the same distribution team would program *The Sound of Music* with *The Texas Chain Saw Massacre*. (Tom Smith, letter to Stephen Ross 01/01/80, WB Fea Pub 0245, SK/15/5/2/4)

The film's release strategy required moving away from the 'platform' approach taken with *2001: A Space Odyssey*, *A Clockwork Orange* and *Barry Lyndon*, which had long runs in major North American cities, relying on audience word of mouth for months before pushing out to general release—this had seen Kubrick's last film commercially flounder, and had even found *2001* slow to profit, taking a decade and the sale of its television rights to break even, according to the filmmaker. Instead, *The Shining* had a limited US release in ten Los Angeles and New York theatres on 23 May 1980—Memorial Day weekend, a popular slot for major studio releases—with a wider release (750 theatres) three weeks later (Hofsess 1980).[11] Releases in the UK (where it was advertised as 'the tide of terror that swept America') and elsewhere followed. A Warner Bros. memo to Kubrick reported packed theatres in preview screenings in Australian cities, with 'extraordinary reactions' from the audience and 'very few negative comments' (Julian Senior, memo to Stanley Kubrick WBFP 118 Shining SK/15/5/2/4), while a local paper in the UK reported 'lots of white faces' exiting a theatre where the film was doing 'very well' despite being moved to a smaller screen (*Buckinghamshire Advertiser*, 9/10/80 SK/15/11/1).

The box office takings in the ten theatres premiering *The Shining* in Los Angeles and New York totalled more than $620,000 for the four day holiday weekend. After ten days, that had grown to $1,168,817. Warner's Executive Vice President Terry Semel told the *New York Times* 'this is the biggest opening our company has ever had in New York and

LA [...] It's bigger than *The Exorcist*, bigger than *Superman* [...] we knew *The Shining* was a major horror-type movie, but a different one, not blood-and-gore [...] We don't see a ceiling for *The Shining*; we think we've got a blockbuster' (in Harmetz 1980). Once the 'tide of terror' had spread to additional theatres, however, its success slowed. Discussing the film in an annual box office review, *Film Comment*'s Myron Miesel suggested 'there was probably no other film this year with stronger box-office elements, or a film of its box-office potential that had fewer commercial goods to deliver [...] It drew torridly for five weeks, then dropped to a pittance for subsequent runs' (in Bingham 1996: 286). *The Shining*, then, might not have been quite the immediate blockbuster Warner Bros. had hoped; *Variety* reported a year after its release that it had taken that time to break even on its $18m production budget plus the costly advertising campaign (Nowell 2011: 193). Yet it continued to bring in audiences. The film grossed nearly $45 million domestically, placing it in the top twenty box-office draws of 1980, and it returned $30.2 million to Warner Bros. in rentals (money made after the exhibitors' profits are removed from box office receipts), the tenth highest such figure in a year when only three films (*The Empire Strikes Back*, *Kramer vs. Kramer* and *The Jerk* [Reiner, 1979]) returned more than $40 million (Prince 2002: 447). By 1983 claims were made that it was among twenty of Warner Bros. most profitable films to date (Norden 1983). Miesel's (and others) complaint that *The Shining* failed to live up to its commercial potential overlooks the release strategy, the average slow climb of Kubrick's films' takings, and the rarity of breakout horror hits. The genre has always had a dedicated audience of horror fans who can ensure minor successes, but often struggles to connect with broader, mainstream audiences turned off by its content. As a result, genuine horror blockbusters are exceptional, occurring around once a decade (Nowell 2014: 132). The mainstream successes of *The Exorcist*, *Rosemary's Baby* and *The Omen* in the years before was evidence of the shift towards meeting the demands of a New Hollywood audience, and the changing regulatory contexts (specifically, the move to the MPAA's age-based ratings system) which enabled such explicit content. The argument that *The Shining* was a commercial disappointment by comparison should be understood alongside its critical reception, which took similar swipes at Kubrick's handling of genre material and his desire for a hit.

RECEPTION AND REAPPRAISAL

Analysis of *The Shining*'s reception reveals that critical and audience responses to the film were mixed; at best the general tone of most reviews could be described as sceptical—marked by incomprehension or indifference—and at worst, the film was 'poorly received'. The reaction is more nuanced than this, however (and the figures do not support any suggestion that audiences universally hated it). Dennis Bingham's valuable case study of *The Shining*'s reception contexts covers the 'confusion and rejection from mainstream reviewers and lukewarm response from audiences' (1996: 286), identifying many of the major issues critics had with the film, and explores the history of its re-evaluation over the fifteen years between its release and Bingham's article. But revisiting the initial reaction, the film's reappraisal (which has continued since the publication of Bingham's study) and its eventual canonisation illuminates the tensions between the commercial and artistic/auteurist expectations for Kubrick's film, and provides some context for understanding *The Shining*'s lasting impact on the genre.

Kubrick's relationship with his critics was famously strained throughout his career, and many of his films, at least since *2001: A Space Odyssey*—which Pauline Kael had labelled 'a monumentally unimaginative movie', and Andrew Sarris 'a disaster' (Hofsess 1980)—had encountered similarly mixed responses. As the filmmaker told *Rolling Stone* in an interview promoting *Full Metal Jacket* in 1987:

> The first reviews of *2001* were insulting, let alone bad. An important Los Angeles critic faulted *Paths of Glory* because the actors didn't speak with French accents. When *Dr. Strangelove* came out, a New York paper ran a review under the head [sic] Moscow could not buy more harm to America. Something like that. But critical opinion on my films has always been salvaged by what I would call subsequent critical opinion. Which is why I think audiences are more reliable than critics, at least initially. Audiences tend not to bring all that critical baggage with them to each film [...] And I really think that a few critics come to my films expecting to see the last film. They're waiting to see something that never happens. (in Cahill 1987)

Bingham attributes this in part to an auteur status which did not easily meet the criteria for understanding auteurist works, with 'interior meaning buried so far beneath the spectacular surfaces [...] Kubrick's films announce themselves as creations, but without the palpable presence of a creator' (1996: 288). This perhaps overestimates the centrality of 'meaningful' elements such as narrative and character in reading Kubrick's films, in turn reducing the significant role of recurring tropes, themes, tone and style in understanding any filmmaker's work from an auteurist approach (arguably especially important to Kubrick's films, where ambiguity and a refusal to simplify or explain for his audience became as much a part of the expectation as his use of parody, or 'spectacular surface' elements such as one-point perspective shots, or meticulously constructed *mise-en-scène*). It does, however, provide some explanation of many influential mainstream critics' hostility toward the filmmaker 'for a battery of reasons: his "no publicity" policy during production, his personal inaccessibility to the American press, his refusal to make his films available for early press screenings, and the paradoxical "self-indulgence" of this absent self' (ibid.). Not that Kubrick seemed to care; 'I don't believe that any critic spends as much time doing his or her work as I do in my work [...] I have never learned anything about my work by reading film critics,' he told the *Washington Post* in an interview to promote *The Shining* (in Hofsess 1980). Neither were his supporters perturbed by the critical resistance to Kubrick's work: 'I was always interested in his relationship with the critics, who always rapped his pictures initially and then three months later they realised they'd seen the greatest film [...] we never had any problems knowing Stanley's movies were great!' (Jack Nicholson, in Pierce 2009: 191).

Kubrick's films were often misunderstood then, and it was common for them to take time to achieve critical recognition. But compounding this was the weight of expectation for both a new Kubrick film—five years since his last, with *Barry Lyndon* then still a 'disappointment' yet to be reappraised—and his first horror film. The anticipation which greeted the film's release was charged by its lengthy production, the recycling of Kubrick interviews in which he expressed a desire to realise his audience's nightmares, and promotion by Diane Johnson, who discussed her and Kubrick's study of Freud and Bettelheim. This all contributed to 'improbable expectations combining hell-raising fright and "poetic genius"' (Bingham 1996: 289). Accordingly, many of the negative reviews (found across tabloid, serious press and academic criticism) found fault in Kubrick's approach to horror, labelling it a 'lame parody' of the genre which failed to provide the scares promised (Jenkins 1997: 71-72), or expressing irritation at the 'portentousness of the film's style applied to formulaic horror material' (Bingham 1996: 290), or its misleading, playful approach to storytelling which miscued audience response (293). Some responses were especially cutting. 'Did Stanley Kubrick really say that *The Shining*, his film of the Stephen King novel, would be the scariest horror movie of all time? He shouldn't have' (Jameson 1980: 28); 'I can't recall a more elaborately ineffective scare movie' (Arnold 1980); '[Kubrick has] flunked the elemental test for a horror film. *The Shining* doesn't scare' (Kauffman, in Bingham 1996: 290). P.L. Titterington, defending the film for *Sight and Sound* in 1981, sympathised with these reactions: 'Judged simply as a horror film, or even a thriller, *The Shining* appears an odd exercise' (117). Even recent academic criticism, while noting the film's conventional blend of 'bloody terror with carnivalistic comedy', argues that Kubrick failed to make the film frightening (Naremore 2007: 203). The reliance on personal response in defining horror, and the subjective nature of film criticism, is emphasised here—because individual critics did not find the film frightening, it was deemed a failure. Elsewhere, more serious analyses of the film—not reviews, but pieces coinciding and chiming with its critical reception—highlight the wilful misunderstanding of the genre by writers who consider it superficial. Fredric Jameson describes *2001* Kubrick's 'supreme technological expertise—as sterile and lobotomized as a trip to the moon', before connecting that to *The Shining*'s 'monotonous and intolerable opening sequence [...] it is possible, of course, that such arid and trivial stretches are essential features of the horror film itself, which (like pornography) finds itself reduced to the empty alternation of shock and the latter's absence' (1981: 117).

There were further issues for critics—including the use of comedy, the puzzling narrative, and the performances ('The crazier Nicholson gets, the more idiotic he looks. Shelley Duvall transforms the warm sympathetic wife of the book into a simpering, semi-retarded hysteric' [*Variety*, 1980]). On a par with the level of complaints over Kubrick's approach to horror were accusations that he had mishandled the adaptation of King's book, a generally well-received bestseller, stripping plot, character and scenes from the source material (Bingham 1996: 290, Jenkins 1997: 69-73). As I have discussed, lamenting things lost is common in the reception of film adaptations, often privileging fidelity over originality while failing to acknowledge changes which might be necessary or even successful—both evident in *The Shining*:

> The dogged belief that an adaptation may triumph only by adhering religiously to its source has been debunked countless times. Moreover, much of the vitriol [...] seems

> somewhat hysterical: Is it true, for example, that Kubrick discarded '90 percent' of the original? Is it universally agreed that the film is less believable than the novel, or that it is incapable of inducing a fright in anyone? While one might argue that the film is flawed in ways that the novel is not, the reverse might also be argued with equal or greater conviction. (Jenkins 1997: 73)

There were some positive reviews which suggested that the film was indeed capable of 'inducing a fright', or that there was much to appreciate in Kubrick's latest movie even if it did confuse or underwhelm audiences looking to be terrified. Positive responses to Nicholson's 'powerful, demonic, spine-chilling performance' (Ian Christie, *Daily Express* 4/10/80 SK/15/11/1) and Duvall's distressed Wendy are balanced against those which found the characters grating on account of 'overacting', and even a number of the more negative reviews praise Kubrick's artistry, attention to detail and technical skill, and the film's music. Significantly, positive reviews or early defences pick up on the film's themes of American family, class and racial tensions, often praising its meanings over and above its expected horror movie experience, or extolling the merits of parody or subversion (Bingham 1996: 291-293).

The Shining faced critical hostility for a number of interconnected reasons. These include an auteurist refusal to connect a serious filmmaker like Kubrick to the supposed trivialities of commercial horror, or conversely, irritation at a perceived snobbery in his artistic approach to its many conventions, subjective responses to what an individual deems 'frightening', a misunderstanding of the purpose of and approach to adapting a successful novel, and the general caution (or bewilderment) that usually greeted Kubrick's work. The divide between mainstream and academic anticipation of Kubrick's film complicate its reception even further:

> Popular film critics in America tended to rake *The Shining* over the coals upon its release because it did not adequately fulfil expectations based on Hollywood convention (some critics complained that it was too complicated and didn't make sense, others that it was too slow, still others that it was not scary enough), while academic film critics apparently steered clear of it because it was a horror film and as such not worth paying attention to. (Smith 1997: 300)

Some positive reviews and the film's box office figures suggest that it was not as universally panned as is often made out, but the various groups anticipating the film—Kubrick devotees, King fans, reviewers, horror fans, mainstream audiences—would have come to the film with varying expectations, and found different causes for celebration or complaint.

The Shining's eventual reappraisal was anticipated by those who were familiar with the evolving critical perceptions of Kubrick's work. P.L. Titterington observed that, as was by then commonplace with each new Kubrick film, *The Shining* required more than one viewing to move beyond the initial reaction of 'bafflement and disappointment' and start making sense of the text and the experience of watching it (1981: 117). Furthermore, they argued that this issue was bound in the tensions between Kubrick's experimental, artistic approach and the commercial potential of his major studio-backed, big budget productions:

> *The Shining* is only properly understood when viewed in this way. Judgement at this stage needs to be tentative, but it can be said that Kubrick is exploring an important direction open to modern cinema that no one else is investigating in quite the same way, and that success would lead to a significant extension of what film can do. In my judgement, he is succeeding. (1981: 121)

The burgeoning academic interest in the film in the first few years following its release, no doubt inspired by these repeated viewings, offered analyses that began to shed light on the film's meanings, as well as its significance (including Jameson 1981, Nelson 1982, Snyder 1982, Cook 1984, Hoile 1984). Critical curiosity grew and *The Shining*'s status began to change through the later part of the decade and in to the 1990s. In 1987, *Rolling Stone*'s interviewer noted the ongoing reappraisal as critics prepared for the release of *Full Metal Jacket*. In 1993, *The New York Times* critic Vincent Canby urged readers to give the film a second chance in a review of another King adaptation, *The Dark Half* (Romero, 1993): 'If you haven't seen *The Shining* recently, rent the video sometime soon. In some eerie fashion, it gets better every year.' By around 1994, Bingham suggests, the film's reception had come 'full circle' (1996: 300) from its initial lacklustre response, to an understanding of it as a significant film. In 2006, Roger Ebert wrote a new review praising *The Shining* and inducting it into his 'Great Movies' collection. His original, negative review can no longer be found on the late critic's otherwise comprehensive website. Collated opinions on websites like Rotten Tomatoes and Metacritic, many taken from positive online reviews published for the film's limited re-releases this decade, evidence this critical about-face.

There are a number of factors which contributed to the shift, in addition to the indifference-reappraisal-celebration patterns of Kubrick criticism. The home video boom of the 1980s, television broadcasts, and eventually DVD releases enabled those multiple repeat viewings which sparked interpretation, changed the context in which it was watched, and awarded the film a new audience—including younger viewers who had not seen *The Shining* in cinemas and were coming at it from a different angle. Various blogs and retrospective reviews heavily rely on memories of seeing *The Shining* on TV or video in the late 1980s and 1990s, describing the effect of first viewings in reverent detail:

> No matter how hard things might become, you can always trust your own perceptions. It's the bottom line, the safety net, the final refuge. It's sanity. Well, that's what I'd always told myself. But when I first saw *The Shining* on TV as a teenager, I felt like I'd been hit by a bus. Or possibly a snow cat. And Jack Nicholson was probably waiting for me behind a door - with an axe.
>
> [...]
>
> The film ended. And as Jack sat frozen in the maze, I sat frozen in a cold sweat to the sofa. I didn't sleep at all that night. My parents came home and I locked my bedroom door, but that wouldn't have stopped Jack. And when I eventually did sleep the next night, it was far from restful then, or for several weeks. Why? Not so much due to scenes of bloody horror, but more because I wasn't really sure what I was seeing, and it took several years for me to understand why. Is this a shared experience, or was I going slightly mad? (Kimpton 2014)[12]

A number of *Room 237*'s subjects nostalgically recollect their first viewings and their delight at finding, in subsequent video and DVD releases, new patterns or confirmed suspicions of things they once thought they had noticed (Mee 2017). Roger Luckhurst describes his own viewing memories of *The Shining* as 'illicit', watching it late with 'patina' (2013: 11). Filmmaker and 'caretaker' of theoverlookhotel.com Lee Unkrich has obsessively rewatched the film countless times since his first viewing at the age of twelve, when it had a profound effect on him, as a child of divorce (2015: 9-10). My own academic interest in *The Shining* grew as I studied film, but was anchored in a childhood obsession with horror movies and intrigue over things I did not quite understand but knew scared me. Memory has proved important to the film's reappraisal, encouraging viewers' return to the film and endless reinterpretations. The shift to digital and the move online has enabled even more obsessive analyses—not just in the availability of a format where the possibilities for rewinding, pausing and rewatching are limitless, but also in the ready availability of extra features like Vivian Kubrick's behind-the-scenes documentary (previously only seen on television around the time of the film's release), or various fansites and forums where theories are exchanged and critiqued, details are pored over, and the film is revered. Over time, *The Shining*'s cult status has grown (and continues to grow) as a result (Egan 2015, Hunter 2016).

The phenomenal success of serious mainstream horror films like *Rosemary's Baby* and *The Exorcist* had, in a way, set *The Shining* up to fail. There was perhaps as much pressure on Kubrick to produce a horror film in keeping with the slick, major studio cycle of the genre's American 'golden age' (as opposed to its gritty independent flicks—just as concerned with similar themes but not operating under the same studio conventions) as there was to produce a great new Kubrick film. While the expectation on Friedkin and Polanski would have been reasonably high—both adapting popular fiction, both critically praised and lauded by the industry (Friedkin had won Directors Guild, Golden Globe and Academy Awards for *The French Connection* in 1971)—both filmmakers were relatively early on in their careers and neither had the same weight of decades worth of reputation and critical interrogation shaping the reception context of their films (Polanski had also by then already had a comparatively minor success in horror with *Repulsion*). Offering neither the narrative simplicity of *Rosemary's Baby* or *The Exorcist*, nor the independent slasher thrills of *Halloween* (the last significantly popular horror film released during *The Shining*'s production) or *Friday the 13th* (Sean S. Cunningham, 1980) (hugely profitable on a low budget, and released just a couple of weeks prior to Kubrick's film), *The Shining* was stuck between not exactly resembling horror which had come before it, and not really meeting the expectations laid out by more immediate trends.

The celebration of horror in the 1970s was rare, and critics soon returned to lambasting the genre and its audiences, as the prominent trends of the 1980s became slashers (often rejected as formulaic, conservative and misogynistic) and sequels (cited as proof of horror's supposed unoriginality). For many, perhaps in the light of these forms which dominated the genre for well over a decade, not to mention the subsequent 'dismal fates' of other poorly received King adaptations (Bingham 1996: 301), the initial judgement of *The Shining* proved to be rather hasty; its re-evaluation coincided with horror's falling out of critical fashion. Eventually, with a new wave of positive criticism, academic analyses, fan obsession and audience appreciation, *The Shining* came to not only be appreciated as a worthy addition to the annals of horror cinema, but as an influential text, the impact of which was felt within the genre, and in time, on popular culture. While many critics, and figures including Stephen King, David Cronenberg (Child 2013) and Brian De Palma (Luckhurst 2013: 8) persist in the argument that Kubrick did not understand the genre he was working in, and treated it with contempt for pure commercial gain, *The Shining* has inspired many others, and 'the eccentricity that initially distinguished the film is now embraced rather than sneered at' (Bingham 1996: 301).

IMPACT AND INFLUENCE

The Shining's influence on the themes, narratives and styles of contemporary horror can be seen across a range of genre texts. Isolated locations, ghosts and haunted houses, and horrible histories have continued to shape horror over the last few decades (as they ever did), while psychic or demonic children are ever-present. Perhaps most obviously, while family dynamics, histories and homes have continued to be configured as a site of terror across cycles and subgenres, the terrible father figure of Jack Torrance brought monstrous patriarchs and fear of fathers and fatherhood to the fore in a genre which, with some notable exceptions (e.g. *The Night of the Hunter* [Laughton, 1955] *Eraserhead*, *The Omen*), has often focused on women and children as the site of familial horror. Powerless fathers (whose ineffectual attempts to assert patriarchal authority often make horrible situations worse for their families) feature in films from *Poltergeist* (Hooper, 1982), *A Nightmare on Elm Street* (Craven, 1984) and *Pet Sematary* (Lambert, 1989) to *28 Weeks Later* (Fresnadillo, 2007), *Sinister* (Derrickson, 2012) and *The Witch*

(Eggers, 2015), but clearer influences can be seen in a number of evil, possessed and/or violent and abusive father figures. Murderous stepfathers terrorise new wives and daughters in *Scream For Help* (Winner, 1984) and *The Stepfather* (Ruben, 1987), which was followed by two sequels and a 2009 remake, while Ryan Reynolds as George Lutz in a new adaptation of *The Amityville Horror* (Douglas, 2005) is subject to comparison with Nicholson as much as with Josh Brolin's original performance. Elsewhere, abusive, murderous fathers in horror draw parallels with Jack Torrance. In *Frailty* (Paxton, 2001), religious fanatic Meiks (Bill Paxton) forces his sons to help kidnap and axe-murder a list of 'sinners' he claims has been handed down to him by an angel. Low-budget British horror *Axed* (Driscoll, 2012) sees a father, frustrated by the loss of his job and his troubled family life, drive his wife and teenagers to a secluded countryside house before terrorising them and chasing his children through the woods with an axe. Chris Cleek (Sean Bridgers) in *The Woman* (McKee, 2011) lacks Torrance's mania and supernatural inspiration, but as the horribly violent head of his long-suffering family, relies on similar dark sitcom parody—played far more for horror than laughs here—to emphasise his misogyny and snide contempt for his wife and daughters. Patriarchal violence merges with the supernatural in *The Messengers* (Pang Brothers, 2007) and *Dream House* (Sheridan, 2011), which both feature mystery storylines about historical murders committed by fathers, and the haunting of families who move in to the homes where these events took place (*Dream House* also references the Grady girls). The absent, alcoholic father of the nightmarish fantasy film *Paperhouse* (Rose, 1988) returns to his daughter's dreamworld as a blinded, monstrous figure who bashes at the eponymous house's front door with a hammer, demanding she let him in, and chastising her for 'playing games'.

The tone and pace of *The Shining*, along with its visual style, played a part in popularising an approach to horror filmmaking which placed an emphasis on creative, artistic and unusual styles with mysterious, puzzle-filled narratives laced with slow-burning, dreadful suspense:

> The film firmly denies us those pleasures that we might expect from a horror film—the pace, like the camera movement, is leisurely, not frenetic; the level of gore is paradoxically restrained and repetitive (in Danny's vision of the girls in the corridor); dialogue is slow and apparently inconsequential at times; and shots are held longer

than we are used to, encouraging (possibly even demanding) that we scan the whole frame for meaning, slowly. (Browning 2009: 199)

As we have seen, Kubrick's film was intended as horror, and toyed with a number of genre expectations in effective new ways, but its unconventional nature had an impact on both its initial response and its eventual reappraisal and ultimate celebration—not that slow and mysterious, or artful, beautiful-looking horror did not already exist, but *The Shining* has had a lasting influence on more recent mainstream releases (as well as arthouse genre films that recollect 'cold' Kubrickian style such as *Under the Skin* [Glazer, 2013]), and some of the most widely seen and well-received horror films of the last few years share similarities that cannot be ignored. *The Babadook* (Kent, 2014), *It Follows* (Mitchell, 2015) and *The Witch* all feature stylistic connections and (very different, female-led) narratives which are vague in approach to motivation and/or resolution, rich in suggestive, psychological and potentially Freudian horrors which prey on viewers' imagination, and supernatural elements which could be—for much of the story at least—interpreted as protagonists' traumatised delusions.

The Babadook deals with the fears and frustrations of single mother Amelia (Essie Davis), who is raising a needy (and slightly creepy) son, Samuel (Noah Wiseman) alone after the accidental death of her husband on the night the boy was born. Sam is convinced of the existence of monsters, including the Babadook, who features in a book which appears, unexplained, on the family's doorstep, and seems to prey on Amelia's repressed grief, sexual frustration and exhaustion. Over time, Amelia becomes delusional, fantasising about killing her son and eventually becoming a physical threat to him. Like *The Shining*, it can be seen as a cautionary tale about the impact of past traumas on families—a comparison Kent felt was fairer to make between her work and King's novel, in which Jack is more sympathetic and his madness explained (MacInnes 2014). Like *The Babadook*, *It Follows*, in which 'It' is a relentless, shapeshifting presence that takes any human form available to endlessly pursue its victim Jay (Maika Monroe), also appears on some level to thematically deal with repressed domestic grief (the death of Jay's father). While owing much to John Carpenter's *Halloween* in its synth score, teen protagonist and suburban setting, its subjective camerawork is arguably closer to the unnerving Steadicam following Danny on his tricycle or encountering Wendy frantically rifling through Jack's novel than it is slasher cinematography. Like those shots (rather than the clear POV that connects us unquestionably to the killer in many slashers), there is an unnerving sense that we are aligned with the perspective of 'It' following, but always a little too far back in a shot held slightly too long, drawing attention to the film's construction. Similarly, there are numerous shots which linger uncomfortably with a central focus—Jay, usually—surrounded by an expanse of nothingness or darkness from which we expect It to appear; given the possibility that the monster could take anyone's form, the most effective of these moments take place in well-lit, public spaces with various extras wandering in the background, coming closer to camera by the second—forcing us, as Browning suggests of *The Shining*, to look in every corner of the frame for meaning. The film seems to be set in an ambiguous time period, with retro eighties styles, mint-condition vintage cars, and digital technology which does not exist (a Kindle-phone hybrid in a plastic clam-shell compact). This adds a level of uncanniness which enhances the strange effect of familiar people (friends, parents) overtaken by It and acting in horrifying ways towards their loved ones. Director Robert Eggers emulated Kubrick in meticulously researching and producing *The Witch*, a seventeenth century-set tale about a puritan family plagued by the supernatural. The film features an atmospheric, creeping dread as the family starts to collapse under the pressure of a failing crop, isolation both figurative and spatial, creepy child twins, sexual repression in their adolescent children, as well as a scene that resembles Jack's seduction by the woman in room 237. Young Caleb (Harvey Scrimshaw) happens across a hut in the woods occupied by a beautiful woman, who steps out of the door and moves towards him in the same slow, purposeful manner as the woman leaves the bath for Jack, embracing him and drawing him in for a kiss, before suddenly changing to her 'real' form, an old witch, who grasps his head as he starts to struggle. The similarities are clear, as Eggers freely acknowledges: 'Sometimes I'm a little disgusted by how much of my film flagrantly reeks of *The Shining*. At the same time, I will admit that if it wasn't for that, I don't think the film would be working for people at all' (in Hall 2016).

Intertextual references which pay homage to *The Shining* are found across the genre; rooms are numbered 237 or the number is otherwise referenced in some abstract way—the time on a clock, or overheard on a radio or in conversation (*Poltergeist*, *Hostel* [Roth, 2005], *Triangle* [Smith, 2009], *The Gift* [Edgerton, 2015], *Get Out* [Peele, 2017]—in which a character also mentions the hedge maze); the bathtub scene is referenced in *Fatal Attraction* (Lyne, 1987), *What Lies Beneath* (Zemeckis, 2000) and in an unmistakeable deep green bathroom in a gothic mansion in *Crimson Peak* (del Toro, 2015); antagonists chop through doors with an axe to get to potential victims in *Friday the 13th Part III* (Miner, 1982), *Children of the Corn* and *The Haunting in Connecticut* (Cornwell, 2009). The ghostly Grady girls feature as one of many potential horrors in *The Cabin in the Woods* (Goddard, 2012), 'Redrum' is referenced in numerous films and is a suitably bloody association for a lipstick shade in *The Neon Demon* (Winding Refn, 2016), and *The Shining*'s opening aerial tracking shot and accompanying music are clearly emulated in the *Cabin Fever* remake (Z, 2016). The genre's debt to Kubrick's film is also obvious on television, as far back as *Twin Peaks* (ABC, 1990-1991), where David Lynch's Kubrick fandom is obvious in the mix of horror and black humour and reliance on the uncanny, the isolated, plush hotel, a murderous father, a puzzling narrative, and a direct quote: 'All work and no play make Ben and Jerry dull boys.' As TV horror has grown in popularity, visual homages have featured in other shows; in a snowy hedge maze complete with a comical frozen corpse in *Scream Queens* (Fox, 2015-present), beautiful replicas of the bathrooms from the Gold Room and 237 in *Hannibal* (NBC, 2013-2015), and the art deco style, patterned carpet, bathroom corpses and ghostly dead children (who ask 'Hello, do you want to play?') of *American Horror Story: Hotel* (FX, 2015-2016).

Beyond horror, *The Shining*'s influence on contemporary popular culture is ever apparent. In film, references feature in comedy (in *Get Him to the Greek* [Stoller, 2010], a character shouts 'It's Kubrickian!' as he is chased down a long hotel corridor), Oscar-winning drama (the labyrinthine hallways on the backstage-theatre set of *Birdman* [Iñárritu, 2014] have the same hexagonal-patterned carpet), science fiction (the deserted spaceship of *Passengers* [Tyldum, 2016] has a bar tended by a red-jacketed, Lloyd-like android) and animation (one of Pixar's main directors is *The Shining* fan Lee Unkrich, who works musical cues, patterns and numerical references into films including *Toy Story 3* [2010]). Homages on TV range from brief quotations ('KDK12' in *Breaking Bad* [AMC, 2008-2013], 'Redrum' in *Daria* [MTV, 1997-2002]), through references to the iconic creepy twin girls in *It's Always Sunny in Philadelphia* [FX, 2005-present] and *30 Rock* [NBC, 2006-2013], to larger sketches, segments and whole episodes devoted to parodying the film (*Spaced* [Channel 4, 1999-2001], *Key and Peele* [Comedy Central, 2012-2015], *Family Guy* [Fox, 1999-present], *South Park* [Comedy Central, 1997-present] and most famously, in *The Simpsons* [Fox, 1989-present] when 'No TV and no beer make Homer go crazy'). Music videos are narratively and stylistically based on *The Shining*, with varying effect—a sleek homage to the Overlook's opulence and doppelgangers in 30 Seconds to Mars's 'The Kill (Bury Me)', and a grimy, gory take on Danny's meeting the Grady girls in Slipknot's 'Spit It Out'. Video games reference 'Redrum' and the film's poster (*Silent Hill*), and a gruesome nod to Nicholson's 'Here's Johnny', which Johnny Cage taunts as he rips through an opponent's ribcage in *Mortal Kombat X*. Premier Inn and Ikea adverts spoof famous sequences, and the iconic hexagonal carpet design features on jewellery, clothing, home furnishings and wallpaper.

Alongside its various direct associations—*Room 237*, the publication of *Doctor Sleep* (and a mooted film adaptation of the sequel), an opera, and rumours of a prequel in production—and various reinterpretations and reimaginings in mashups and fan videos (a trailer recut to make *The Shining* look like a family comedy, a 'Grand Overlook' trailer which juxtaposes shots from Kubrick's film with those taken from *The Grand Budapest Hotel* [Wes Anderson 2014], highlighting some striking visual similarities, and a short film which imagines the outcome of David Lynch directing the movie),[13] pervasive allusions to *The Shining* are still commonplace in the cultural psyche of the twenty-first century, almost forty years after its release. For some, its retirement is long overdue:

> [...] You could barely post a photo of a corridor on social media without some wag responding with 'REDRUM', or a tricycle-related quip, or 'Watch out for the twins!' – as though there were no other corridors in the movies, or indeed in life. I became fed up with the ubiquity of the film's tropes, the endless quotation and recycling, and started seeing its flaws [...] and the underlying sense of an A-list director slumming it in a genre he essentially despises. (Billson 2016)

Kubrick's 'slumming it' is, as we have seen, readily disproved, and I disagree with Billson, who goes on to complain that 'the only emotion in *The Shining* is the "Gotcha!" of a fairground haunted mansion', whose 'thrills have long since been parsed into extinction'. The persistent references to the film are evidence of enduring appeal and its deep effect on horror cinema and beyond. While many of its tropes became clichés through repetition long ago, its impact is ever-present as the genre continues to evolve, grow, and often thrive in the texts that embrace it.

FOOTNOTES

11. This wider release excluded a final scene in which Ullman visits Wendy and Danny in hospital, which was cut by Kubrick after the opening weekend.
12. See also: Chestnutcafe (2017); Smith, Ellie Wilkin (2014); Young, Joshua (2013).
13. '*The Shining* Recut' (neochosen, 2006), https://www.youtube.com/watch?v=KmkVWuP_sO0, 'Wes Anderson's *The Shining*' (Steve Ramsden Unexplored Films, 2015), https://www.youtube.com/watch?v=Nsi06PG7w_0, 'Blue Shining' (Richard Vezina, 2015), https://vimeo.com/129938191,

Conclusion

The Shining's reception was no doubt impacted by commercial expectation, Kubrick's critical reputation (both as a filmmaking genius and a controversial brand name whose work often puzzled reviewers), and its unusual aesthetic approach to the horror genre. The suggestion that critics who did not understand the film or its appeal struggled because they had 'stupidly labelled it' a (failed) horror film (Mamber 1991, quoted in Bingham 1996: 286) is a reiteration of the idea that *The Shining* should not be considered as part of the genre, and that Kubrick was working outside of it; as I have argued, neither is particularly true. Working faster than the critical reappraisal which picked up steam over time and alongside rereleases in the video and then digital age, horror cinema seemed to more swiftly (and more keenly) assimilate its various tropes, styles and references, filmmakers perhaps recognising *The Shining*'s potential longevity and various contributions to the genre over critics approaching foremost it as 'a Stanley Kubrick film'.

Working with Diane Johnson, Kubrick skilfully adapted King's novel, streamlining an overstuffed backstory and simplifying characters, motivation and plot to suit the film form, taking the opportunity to unnerve a wide audience with varying beliefs by leaving supernatural and psychological horrors open to interpretation, and refusing the neat resolutions of the novel. King's and Kubrick's versions of the Torrances' story have different functions, and, to butcher an old adage, we should never judge a film by its book. Kubrick was also adapting horror from within its parameters—deconstructing it while playing with its aesthetic and thematic conventions, setting a new tone and style, and paving the way for its development by introducing tropes which would become part of the genre's iconography through their eventual repetition. The use of parody, rather than Kubrick mocking the genre and poking fun at horror audiences, can instead be understood as part of this development. Not only does it shade *The Shining* with an uncomfortable black humour which serves to enhance its horrors, but self-reflection, satire and parody have long been considered as part of a series of stages which help to shape genre development (Schatz 1981, Giannetti 1999). Genres thrive on patterns of sameness and difference, and evolve through the introduction of new forms which both reflect and build on what came before. They are not 'inherently static', despite the repetition of their conventions, but can instead be seen as processes 'marked fundamentally by difference, variation, and change' (Neale 1990: 56).

Similarly, the themes at the heart of the film's narrative are both conventional to the genre and contribute to its development, centralising repressed patriarchal rage, isolation and madness, and using the Overlook's ghosts to tie these to historical horrors which have continued to haunt us:

> Kubrick's characters may not be unlike the members of his audience, who, provided with a story ostensibly about the mental breakdown of an isolated man and the collapse of his family, are actually given a tale about the hidden brutality of their own institutions, an uncanny fable mirroring their own pursuit of mastery and their own subjection to the nightmare of history. (Lutz 2010: 177)

Lutz's argument is fair, but the two tales under discussion are not mutually exclusive, and all of these commentaries are present in the film. *The Shining* is not about *either* breakdown, isolation and the family *or* a deeper, uncanny reflection of deep-seated troubles in American institutions throughout history. It is about all of these and more, and the threads which bind together patriarchal violence, the collapse of the nuclear family, systemic racism and class tensions, and the danger of looking nostalgically at a bygone era, are what make the film so effective. The threat of the cyclical repetition of violence is horrifying, at whichever level the audience chooses to pitch their reading of the film's themes. Just as the balance between supernatural and psychological terror is left for viewers to discern, so too can we make our own meanings—infuriating some and thrilling others. Theories on *The Shining*'s 'true meaning' which seek to elevate it above the horror genre miss an important point. Its multiple possible interpretations, rather than providing evidence for why it should be excluded from considerations of genre and industry, have the absolute opposite effect. Horror studies have always sought to move beyond codes and conventions—looking past iconography to consider the genre's deeper ideological meanings, political intentions, and psychological effects, and horror films have often acted (and been understood) as vehicles for social commentary.

The chapters in this book have approached some of the common contexts for understanding *The Shining*—as a Kubrick film and as an adaptation, analysing themes and meanings and reflecting on its reception—but have done so from the categorical position that it is a *horror film*, and deserves analysis as such. While many studies and critiques have continued to limit its status within the genre, audiences and filmmakers have embraced *The Shining*, with all of its ambiguities and oddities, as an enduringly popular, effective horror film. It marked a turning point in horror cinema's history, and confirmed that mainstream, commercial genre films could be smart, beautiful and original. It was stylistically and tonally unusual, auteurist and technically accomplished, enigmatic and unapologetic, and its influence is evident in a range of subsequent works. Over time, it has continued to inspire artistic, atmospheric horror, and its endless recycled references have contributed to both its extraordinary impact on popular culture, and its ultimate genre canonisation. *The Shining* has staked its claim in horror history, where it will stay… forever and ever.

16 *'You have always been the caretaker'*

BIBLIOGRAPHY

Abrams, N. (2014) 'The Banalities of Evil: Polanski, Kubrick, and the Reinvention of Horror' in Ungureanu, C, and Bradatan, C. (eds) *Religion in Contemporary European Cinema*. Abingdon: Taylor and Francis. 145-164.

Allen, G. (2015) 'The Unempty Wasps' Nest: Kubrick's *The Shining*, adaptation, chance, interpretation', *Adaptation* Vol 8, No. 3. 361-371.

Arnold, G. (1980) 'Kubrick's $12 Million Shiner', *The Washington Post*, June 13. https://www.washingtonpost.com/archive/lifestyle/1980/06/13/kubricks-12-million-shiner/1159d306-6c4e-4ba1-b0dd-3f39d3b947e1/?utm_term=.85a723b40baf. Accessed 20/02/17.

Baxter, J. (1997) 'Kubrick in Hell' in Olsen, D. (ed.) (2015) *Stanley Kubrick's The Shining: Studies in the Horror Film*. Lakewood: Centipede Press. 15-54.

BBC (2004) 'Shining named perfect scary movie', August 9. http://news.bbc.co.uk/1/hi/entertainment/3537938.stm Accessed 06/07/16.

BBC (2013) 'Stephen King returns to The Shining with Doctor Sleep', September 19. http://www.bbc.co.uk/news/entertainment-arts-24151957 Accessed 07/08/16.

Billson, A. (2016) 'The Shining has lost its shine – Kubrick was slumming it in a genre he despised', *The Guardian*, October 27. https://www.theguardian.com/film/2016/oct/27/stanley-kubrick-shining-stephen-king. Accessed 01/11/16.

Bingham, D. (1996) 'The Displaced Auteur: A Reception History of *The Shining*' in Falsetto, M. (ed) *Perspectives on Stanley Kubrick*. New York: G K Hall. 284-306.

Bozung, J. (2015) 'Joe Turkel: Interview' in Olsen, D. (ed.) *Stanley Kubrick's The Shining: Studies in the Horror Film*. Lakewood: Centipede Press. 377-391.

Brophy, P. (1986) 'Horrality—The Textuality of Contemporary Horror Films', *Screen* Vol 27, No 1. 2-13.

Browning, M. (2009) *Stephen King on the Big Screen*. Bristol: Intellect.

Cahill, T. (1987) 'The Rolling Stone Interview: Stanley Kubrick in 1987', *Rolling Stone*. http://www.rollingstone.com/culture/news/the-rolling-stone-interview-stanley-kubrick-in-1987-20110307. Accessed 07/10/16.

Canby, V. (1993) 'Pseudonym Comes to Life in a Stephen King Tale', *The New York Times*, April 23. http://www.nytimes.com/movie/review?res=9F0CE0DF1630F930A15757C0A965958260. Accessed 05/02/17.

Carnicke, S. M. (2006) 'The Material Poetry of Acting: "Objects of Attention", Performance Style and Gender in The Shining and Eyes Wide Shut', *Journal of Film and Video*, Vol. 58, No. 1/2. 21-29.

Cherry, B. (2009) *Horror*. Abingdon: Routledge.

Chestnutcafe (2017) 'The Shining'. January 10. https://www.chess.com/blog/Chessnutcafe/the-shining. Accessed 11/08/17.

Child, B. (2013) 'David Cronenberg: Stanley Kubrick didn't understand horror', *The Guardian*. November 5. https://www.theguardian.com/film/2013/nov/05/david-cronenberg-stanley-kubrick-horror-the-shining. Accessed 15/03/17.

Ciment, M. (1980) 'Stanley Kubrick: Interview' in Olsen, D. (ed.) (2015) *Stanley Kubrick's The Shining: Studies in the Horror Film*. Lakewood: Centipede Press. 473-502.

Clover, C. J. (1992) *Men Women and Chainsaws: Gender in the Modern Horror Film* Princeton: Princeton University Press.

Cocks, G. (2004) *The Wolf at the Door: Stanley Kubrick, History and the Holocaust*. New York: Peter Lang.

Cook, D. A. (1984) 'American Horror: The Shining' *Literature/Film Quarterly* Vol 12, No. 1. 2-4.

Cook, D. A. (2002) *Lost Illusions: American Cinema in the Shadow of Vietnam and Watergate*. Berkeley: University of California Press.

Cramer, S. (1997) 'Cinematic Novels and 'Literacy' Films: The Shining in the Context of the Modern Horror Film', in Cartmell, D., I.Q. Hunter, H. Kaye and I. Whelehan (eds) *Trash Aesthetics: Popular Culture and its Audience*. London: Pluto Press. 132-142.

Dickstein, M. (2004) 'The Aesthetics of Fright' in B.K. Grant and C. Sharrett (eds) *Planks of Reason: Essays on the Horror Film*. Lanham: Scarecrow Press. 50-63.

Ebert, R. (2006) 'Review: The Shining', June 18. http://www.rogerebert.com/reviews/great-movie-the-shining-1980 Accessed 07/02/17.

Egan, K. (2015) 'Precious footage of the auteur at work: Framing, accessing, using, and cultifying Vivian Kubrick's Making The Shining', *New Review of Film and Television Studies*, Vol. 13, No. 1. 63-82.

Falsetto, M. (ed) (1996) *Perspectives on Stanley Kubrick*. New York: G K Hall.

Fleming Jr, M. (2016) 'Stephen King On What Hollywood Owes Authors When Their Books Become Films: Q&A', *Deadline*, February 2. http://deadline.com/2016/02/stephen-king-what-hollywood-owes-authors-when-their-books-become-films-q-a-the-dark-tower-the-shining-1201694691/ Accessed 07/08/16.

Gelder, K. (ed.) (2000) *The Horror Reader*. London: Routledge.

Gengaro, C. (2013) 'Midnight, The Stars and You: The Music of The Shining' in in Olsen, D. (ed.) (2015) *Stanley Kubrick's The Shining: Studies in the Horror Film*. Lakewood: Centipede Press. 167-217.

Giannetti, L. (1999) *Understanding Movies*. London: Longman.

Greene, A. (2014) 'Stephen King: The Rolling Stone Interview', *Rolling Stone*, October 31. http://www.rollingstone.com/culture/features/stephen-king-the-rolling-stone-interview-20141031?page=5. Accessed 07/08/16.

Hall, J. (2016) 'The Influences of "The Witch" Part One: Director Robert Eggers on 'The Shining", */Film*. February 16. http://www.slashfilm.com/the-witch-influences-the-shining/. Accessed 02/03/17.

Harmetz, A. (1980) 'Shining and Empire set records', *New York Times*, May 28. Accessed in SK/15/5/2/4, Stanley Kubrick Archives, University of the Arts London.

Hills, M. (2005) *The Pleasures of Horror*. London: Continuum.

Hofsess, J. (1980) 'The Shining', *The Washington Post*, June 1st. https://www.washingtonpost.com/archive/lifestyle/1980/06/01/the-shining/2f44872d-260b-4ec9-8384-74b7bae90303/?utm_term=.59e9ce90ae27. Accessed 07/02/17.

Hoile, C. (1984) 'The Uncanny and the fairy tale in Kubrick's The Shining', *Literature/Film Quarterly* Vol. 12. No. 1. 5-12.

Humphries, R. (2002) *The American Horror Film: An Introduction*. Edinburgh: Edinburgh University Press.

Hunter, I.Q. (2015) 'Introduction: Kubrick and Adaptation', *Adaptation* Vol. 8, No. 3. 277–282.

Hunter, I.Q. (2016) *Cult Film as a Guide to Life*. London: Bloomsbury.

Hutchings, P. (2004) *The Horror Film*. Abingdon: Taylor and Francis.

Jacobsen, M. (2013) '"I Know What The Shining Is Really About" Inside the Crowded Cult at the Overlook Hotel', *Vulture*, March 17. http://www.vulture.com/2013/03/the-shining-cult-at-the-overlook-hotel.html. Accessed 07/04/13.

Jameson, F. (1981) 'The Shining', *Social Text* No. 4. 114-125.

Jameson, R.T. (1980) 'Kubrick's Shining', *Film Comment* Vol. 16 No. 4. 28-32.

Jancovich, M. (1994) *American Horror From 1951* Staffordshire: Keele University Press.

Jancovich, M. (ed.) (2002) *Horror: The Film Reader*. Abingdon: Routledge.

Jenkins, G. (1997) *Stanley Kubrick and the Art of Adaptation: Three Novels, Three Films*. Jefferson: McFarland.

Johnson, D. (2006) 'Writing The Shining' in Cocks, G., Diedrick, J. and Perusek, G. (eds) *Depth of Field: Stanley Kubrick, Film and the Uses of History*. Madison: University of Wisconsin Press. 55-61.

Jones, A. (2005) *The Rough Guide to Horror Movies*. London: Rough Guides.

Kellner, D. and Ryan, M. (1988) *Camera Politica: The Politics and Ideology of Contemporary Hollywood Film*. Bloomington: Indiana University Press.

Keeler, G. (1981) 'The Shining: Ted Kramer has a Nightmare', *Journal of Popular Film and Television*. Vol. 8, No. 4. 2-8.

Kennedy, H. (1980) 'Kubrick Goes Gothic', *American Film*. Vol. 5 No. 8. 49-52.

Kimpton, P. (2014) 'The Shining: the film that frightened me most', *The Guardian*, October 24. https://www.theguardian.com/film/2014/oct/24/the-shining-the-film-that-frightened-me-most. Accessed 20/03/17.

King, S. (1977) *The Shining*. London: Hodder & Stoughton. Reprinted 2011.

King, S. (2013) *Doctor Sleep*. London: Hodder & Stoughton.

Kolker, R. (2011) *A Cinema of Loneliness: Penn, Stone, Kubrick, Scorsese, Spielberg, Altman*. Oxford: Oxford University Press.

Kroll, J. (1980) 'Stanley Kubrick's Horror Show' *Newsweek Magazine*. June 2. 52-54.

Leigh, D. (2017) 'Eraserhead: the true story behind David Lynch's surreal shocker', *The Guardian*, March 22. https://www.theguardian.com/film/2017/mar/22/david-lynch-eraserhead. Accessed 07/01/17.

Lightman, H. (1980) 'Photographing Stanley Kubrick's the Shining', *American Cinematographer*. Vol. 61. Issue 8. 780-844.

LoBrutto, V. (1997) *Stanley Kubrick*. London: Faber and Faber.

Luckhurst, R. (2013) *The Shining* London: BFI.

Lutz, J. (2010) 'From Domestic Nightmares to the Nightmare of History: Uncanny Eruptions of Violence in King's and Kubrick's Versions of The Shining', in Fahy, T. (ed.). *The Philosophy of Horror*. Lexington: University Press of Kentucky. 161-178.

MacInnes, P. (2014) 'The Babadook: "I wanted to talk about the need to face darkness in ourselves"', *The Guardian*. October 18. https://www.theguardian.com/film/2014/oct/18/the-babadook-jennifer-kent Accessed 02/03/17.

Magistrale, T. (1998) *Discovering Stephen King's The Shining*. Rockville: Wildside Press.

Magistrale, T. (2003) *Hollywood's Stephen King*, New York: Palgrave Macmillan.

Manchel, F. (1995) 'What about Jack? Another Perspective on Family Relationships in Stanley Kubrick's The Shining', *Literature/Film Quarterly*, Vol. 23, No. 1. 68-78.

Mayersberg, P. (1980) 'The Overlook Hotel', in Falsetto, M. (1996) *Perspectives on Stanley Kubrick*. New York: G K Hall. 253-259.

McAvoy, C. (2015) 'The Uncanny, the gothic and the loner: Intertextuality in the adaptation process of The Shining', *Adaptation* Vol. 8 No. 3. 345-360.

McAvoy, C. (2015b) 'Diane Johnson: Interview' in Olsen, D. (ed.) *Stanley Kubrick's The Shining: Studies in the Horror Film*. Lakewood: Centipede Press. 533-566.

McAvoy, C. (2015c) 'Creating The Shining: Looking Beyond the Myths', in Kramer, P., Ljujic, T., and Daniels, R. (eds) *Stanley Kubrick: New Perspectives*. London: Black Dog Publishing.

Mee, L. (2017) 'Room 237: Cinephilia, History and Adaptation' in Kay, J.B., Mahoney, C. and Shaw, C. (eds), *The Past in Visual Culture: Essays on Memory, Nostalgia and the Media*. McFarland: Jefferson. 154-169.

Metz, W. (1997) 'Toward a Post-structural Influence in Film Genre Study: Intertextuality and The Shining', *Film Criticism*, Vol. 22, No. 1. 38-90.

Mitchell, N. (2013) *Carrie (Devil's Advocates)*. Leighton Buzzard: Auteur.

Model, K. (2012) 'Gender Hyperbole and the Uncanny in the Horror Film: The Shining', in Gledhill, C. (ed.). *Gender Meets Genre in Postwar Cinemas*. Champaign: University of Illinois Press.

Murakami, S. (2013) 'Unearthing how horror affects the heart', *Huffington Post*, November 11. http://www.huffingtonpost.co.uk/shingo-murakami/unearthing-how-horror-affects-the-heart_b_4234690.html. Accessed 06/07/16.

Naremore, J. (2006) 'Stanley Kubrick and the Aesthetics of the Grotesque' *Film Quarterly*. Vol. 60, No. 1. 4-14.

Naremore, J. (2007) *On Kubrick*. London: BFI.

Neale, S. (1990) 'Questions of Genre', *Screen*, Vol. 31 No. 1. 45-66.

Nelson, T.A. (1982) *Kubrick: Inside a Film Artist's Maze*. Bloomington: Indiana University Press.

Newman, K. (1988) *Nightmare Movies*. London: Bloomsbury.

Nolan, A. (2011) 'Seeing is Digesting: Labyrinths of Historical Ruin in Stanley Kubrick's The Shining', *Cultural Critique*. Vol. 77. 180-204.

Norden, E. (1983) 'Stephen King, June 1983', *50 Years of the Playboy Interview: Stephen King*, Playboy Enterprises (ebook) 2012.

Nowell, R. (2011) *Blood Money: A History of the First Teen Slasher Film Cycle*. London: Continuum.

Nowell, R. (2014) '"A kind of Bacall quality" Jamie Lee Curtis, Stardom, and Gentrifying non-Hollywood Horror' in Nowell, R. (ed.) *Merchants of Menace: The Business of Horror Cinema*. London: Bloomsbury.

Okorafor, N. (2004) 'Stephen King's Super-Duper Magical Negroes', *Strange Horizons* October 25 http://strangehorizons.com/non-fiction/articles/stephen-kings-super-duper-magical-negroes/. Accessed 10/01/17.

Olsen, D. (ed.) (2015) *Stanley Kubrick's The Shining: Studies in the Horror Film*. Lakewood: Centipede Press.

Penner, J., Schneider, S.J. and Duncan, P. (2008) *Horror Cinema*. Köln: Taschen.

Pezzotta, E. (2013) *Stanley Kubrick: Adapting the Sublime* Jackson: University Press of Mississippi.

Phillips, K. R. (2005) *Projected Fears: Horror Films and American Culture*. Westport: Praeger.

Pierce, N. (2009) 'All work and no play: Jack Nicholson on the making of The Shining', *Empire*. June. Issue 240. 188-195.

Prince, S. (2002) *A New Pot of Gold: Hollywood under the Electronic Rainbow*. Berkeley: University of California Press.

Prince, S. (2004) (ed.) *The Horror Film*. New Brunswick: Rutgers University Press.

Robinson, T. (2013) 'What The Shining miniseries reveals about the King/Kubrick divide'. *The Dissolve*. October 31. https://thedissolve.com/features/movie-of-the-week/248-what-the-shining-miniseries-reveals-about-the-king/. Accessed 15/02/17.

Schatz, T. (1981) *Hollywood Genres: Formulas, Filmmaking and the Studio System*. New York: Random House.

Schauer, B. and Bordwell, D. (2006) 'A Hollywood Timeline, 1960-2004' in Bordwell, D. *The Way Hollywood Tells It*. Berkeley: University of California Press. 191-242.

Schneider, S. J. (ed.) (2009) *101: Horror Movies You Must See Before You Die*. London: Quintessence.

Smith, E.W. (2014) 'I Used to Hate The Shining: A Confessional'. October 14. https://stnlykbrk.wordpress.com/2014/10/13/i-used-to-hate-the-shining-an-exploration-into-the-shining-as-an-anti-horror/. Accessed 11/08/17.

Smith, G. (1997) "Real Horrorshow": The juxtaposition of subtext, satire and audience implication in Stanley Kubrick's The Shining', *Literature/Film Quarterly* Vol. 25, No. 4. 300-306.

Snyder, S. (1982) 'Family Life and Leisure Culture in The Shining', *Film Criticism* Vol.7, No.1. 4-13.

Sobchack, V. (1996) 'Bringing it all back home: Family economy and generic exchange' in Grant, B.K. (ed.) *The Dread of Difference: Gender and the Horror Film*. Austin: University of Texas Press. 143-163.

Thorne, R. (2014) *Cult Horror* London: Flame Tree.

Titterington, P.L. (1981) 'Kubrick and The Shining', *Sight and Sound* Vol. 50 No.2. 117-121.

Trigg, D. (2015) 'Archaeologies of Hauntings: Phenomenology and Psychoanalysis in The Shining' in Olsen, D. (ed.) *Stanley Kubrick's The Shining: Studies in the Horror Film*. Lakewood: Centipede Press. 273-292.

Tudor, A. (1989) *Monsters and Mad Scientists: A Cultural History of the Horror Movie*. Oxford: Basil Blackwell.

Unkrich, L. (2015) in Olsen, D. (ed.) *Stanley Kubrick's The Shining: Studies in the Horror Film.* Lakewood: Centipede Press. 9-12.

Variety (1980) 'Review, The Shining' http://variety.com/1979/film/reviews/the-shining-1200424592/. Accessed 20/02/17.

Webster, P. (2011) *Love and Death in Kubrick: A Critical Study of the Films from Lolita through Eyes Wide Shut.* Jefferson: McFarland.

Wells, P. (2000) *The Horror Genre From Beelzebub to Blair Witch.* London: Wallflower.

Wollen, P. (1963) *Signs and Meaning in the Cinema,* London: BFI. Reprinted 1998.

Wood, R. (1979) 'An Introduction to the American Horror Film' in Britton, A. et al. (eds) *The American Nightmare: Essays on the Horror Film.* Toronto: Festival of Festivals.

Wood, R. (2003) *Hollywood from Vietnam to Reagan...And Beyond* (Expanded and Revised Edition). New York: Columbia University Press.

Worland, R. (2007) *The Horror Film: An Introduction.* Oxford: Blackwell.

Wright, J. D. (2011) 'Shades of Horror: Fidelity and Genre in Stanley Kubrick's The Shining', in MacCabe, C., Murray, K. and Warner, R. *True to the Spirit.* Oxford: Oxford University Press. 173-201.

Young, Joshua (2013) 'Happy Memory: The Shining'. March 31. http://totorovsbatman.blogspot.co.uk/2013/03/happy-memory-shining-also-one.html. Accessed 11/08/17.

DEVIL'S ADVOCATES

"Auteur Publishing's new Devil's Advocates critiques on individual titles offer bracingly fresh perspectives from passionate writers. The series will perfectly complement the BFI archive volumes." Christopher Fowler, Independent on Sunday

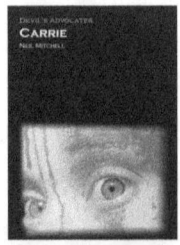

CARRIE – NEIL MITCHELL

"Top notch... intelligent... insightful." – Total Film

"... [goes] into exhaustive detail on the genesis of the film... a brisk, enjoyable read. *****" – Frightfest.co.uk

HALLOWEEN – MURRAY LEEDER

"Murray Leeder's thoughtful, clearly expressed analysis is far reaching in scope while resisting the temptation to become sidetracked... a joy to read; it's insightful and well researched and serves as an encouragement to return to Halloween once again" – Exquisite Terror

SUSPIRIA – ALEXANDRA HELLER-NICHOLAS

"... at once original and deeply subversive... This is a really sharp book, and an excellent series... Brief, compact, and authoritative, these are the volumes to beat on these classic genre films." – Wheeler Winston Dixon

THE TEXAS CHAIN SAW MASSACRE – JAMES ROSE

"[James Rose] find[s] new and unusual perspectives with which to address [the] censor-baiting material. Unsurprisingly, the effect... is to send the reader back to the films... watch the films, read these Devil's Advocates analyses of them." – Crime Time

www.ingramcontent.com/pod-product-compliance
Lightning Source LLC
Chambersburg PA
CBHW071850230426
43671CB00012B/2140